General Editor
David Piper

Velázquez

Every Painting

Nicola Spinosa

Vice-President, Galleria Nazionale di Capodimonte;
Professor of Art History, University of Cosenza

translated by Catherine Atthill

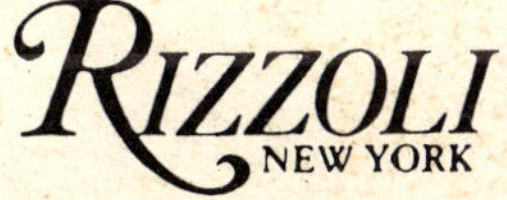

Foreword by the General Editor

Several factors have made possible the phenomenal surge of interest in art in the twentieth century: notably the growth of museums, the increase of leisure, the speed and relative ease of modern travel, and not least the extraordinary expansion and refinement of techniques of reproduction of works of art, from the ubiquitous colour postcards, cheap popular books of colour plates, to film and television. A basic need – for the general art public, as for specialized students, academic libraries, the art trade – is for accessible, reliable, comprehensive accounts of the works of the individual great masters of painting; this has not been met since the demise before 1939 of the famous German series, *Klassiker der Kunst*; when such accounts do appear, in the shape of full *catalogues raisonnés*, they are vast in price as in size, and beyond the reach of most individual pockets and the capacity of most private bookshelves.

The aim of the present series is to provide an up-to-date equivalent of the *Klassiker* for the now enormously enlarged public interested in art. Each volume (or volumes, where the quantity of work to be reproduced cannot be contained in a single one) catalogues and illustrates chronologically the complete paintings of the artist concerned. The catalogues reflect as far as possible a consensus of current expert opinion about the status of each picture; in the nature of things, consensus has yet to be reached on many points, and no one professionally involved in the study of art-history would ever be so rash as to claim definitiveness. Within the bounds of human fallibility, however, every effort has been made to achieve both comprehensiveness and factual accuracy, while the quality of reproduction aimed at is the highest possible in this price range, and includes, of course, colour. Every effort has also been made to hold the price down to the lowest possible level, so that these volumes may stay within the reach not only of libraries, but of the individual student and lover of great painting, so that they may gradually accumulate their own 'Museum without Walls'. The introductions, written by acknowledged authorities, summarize the life and works of the artists, while the illustrations place in perspective the complete story of the development of each painter's genius through his career.

David Piper

Introduction

Diego Velázquez was born in Seville on 6 June 1599, the son of João Rodriguez de Silva and Jerónima Velázquez, both members of families of Portuguese origin from Oporto. In official documents, as was then customary in Spain, the painter always referred to himself as Diego de Silva Velázquez, using both father's and mother's surnames. A small number of his paintings are signed, either Diego Velázquez (the name by which he was known in contemporary writings) or, towards the end of his life, Diego de Silva.

According to Palomino, though there are no documents to bear this out, he started his apprenticeship as a painter in the workshop of Francisco Herrera the Elder as a boy of ten. However, by 1 December 1610 he had moved to Francisco Pacheco's workship. On 27 September 1611 Pacheco signed a contract with his father João, agreeing to train the boy in six years. At the end of this time young Velázquez was examined by Pacheco and by Juan de Uceda. On 14 March 1617 he was admitted into the Seville painters' guild which meant he could exercise his profession freely anywhere in the kingdom of Spain. Pacheco, his teacher, was not an outstanding artist, but he had a firm grasp of the rudiments of the late Mannerist style and surprisingly was a keen admirer of Caravaggio, though he may only have known his work at second hand. Velázquez' apprenticeship obviously played an important part in his development and early mature works, but it also taught him an approach to his art which stood him in good stead when he reached stylistic maturity. Pacheco soon noticed his pupil's outstanding gifts. He always took an affectionate interest in his progress and showed this by giving him his daughter Juana in marriage in April 1618. From Pacheco Velázquez received a sound basic training in the discipline of drawing models taken from the great painters of the Italian Cinquecento and in the composition of objects taken from life and copied in minute detail. This training, with its Renaissance bias, was to prove valuable as a means of transmuting images taken from real life into forceful artistic solutions which are always unfailingly three-dimensional and visually convincing.

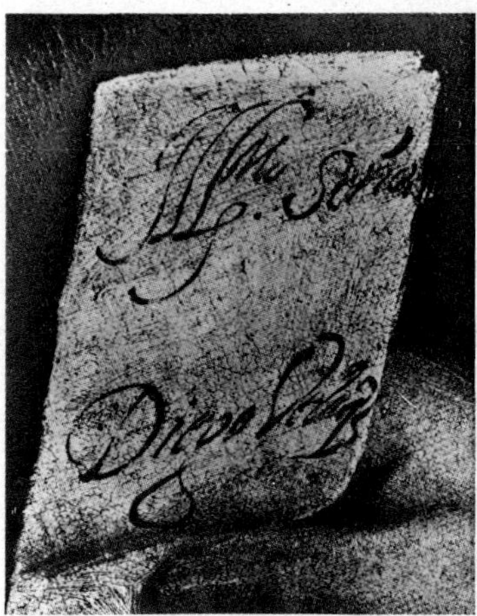

One of the rare surviving examples of Velázquez' signature from Hand of an Ecclesiastic *(No. 79).*

These qualities are already apparent in the group of canvases which the young artist painted between 1618 and 1629 in Seville and soon after his final move to Madrid. Vigorous, three-dimensional, powerfully expressive but never unrestrained, these paintings are outstanding examples of the naturalistic trend in European art at the beginning of the seventeenth century.

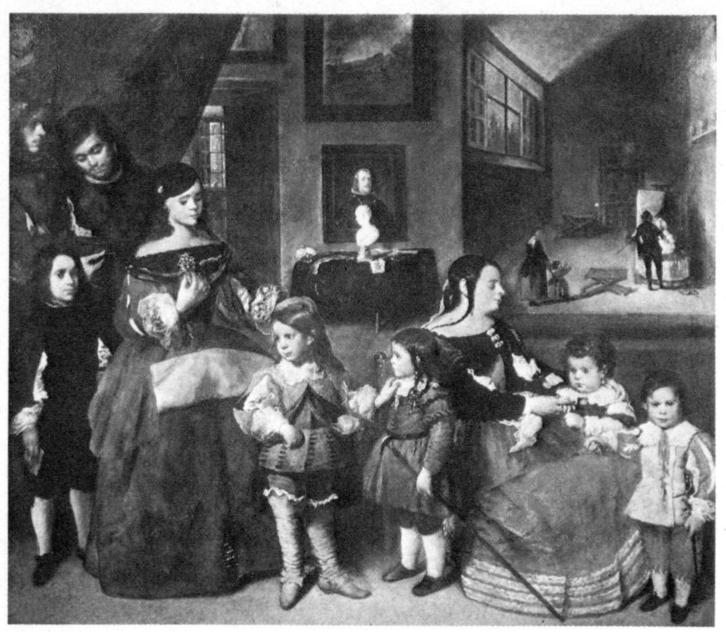

The group consists of several different styles of painting: a series of genre paintings or *bodegones* with figures (the earliest known example is the *Old Woman frying Eggs* dated 1618 (No. 12), sometimes with religious scenes inserted in the background (*Christ at Emmaus* (No. 10), and *Christ in the House of Martha and Mary* (No. 16); several paintings of purely religious subjects (*St John writing the Apocalypse* (No. 3) and *The Immaculate Conception* (No. 4), *The Adoration of the Magi* (No. 7), and *Christ at Emmaus* (No. 22)); and finally a fairly large number of exceptionally fine portraits which can be reliably dated between 1620 and 1624–5 (from *Cristóbal Suárez de Ribera* (No. 18) in Seville and *Doña Jerónima de la Fuente* (No. 19) in the Prado to the bust of *Philip IV* (No. 27) in Dallas and the full-length portrait of him (No. 29) in the Metropolitan, New York, or the two portraits of *Olivares* in São Paulo, Brazil (No. 30) and New York (No. 31)). These paintings, especially the earlier ones, are mainly concerned with the portrayal of everyday figures and situations, images of popular life sharply depicted with marked chiaroscuro contrasts, and a skilful balancing of mass, yet filled with a sense of human involvement. It is certainly tempting to regard them as evidence of the influence on Velázquez of Caravaggio or one of the many *Caravaggisti*, both Italian and North European, who followed in the master's footsteps in Rome before 1615.

However, there is no evidence that Velázquez knew Caravaggio's work during his time in Seville, though Palomino suggests he did. It seems likely that he did not encounter Caravaggio's work at first hand until his move to Madrid and his visits to Italy, but by then he had already reached a level of artistic maturity which would have made it difficult for him to absorb much from Caravaggio's approach. The works he painted during his Seville period and soon after his move to Madrid show a concern with capturing natural detail. But, as Lafuente Ferrari has rightly pointed out, this concern – evident in the vigorous handling of forms seen in direct light against the painting's background, the painstaking transcription of detail, the refusal to leave out any element of reality – is not

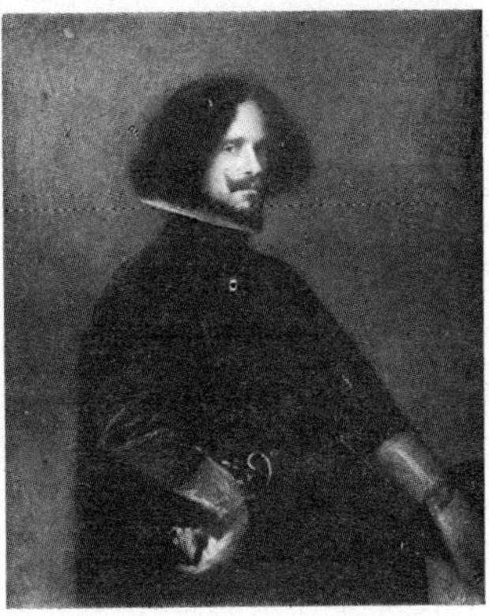

Left, The Family of the Artist *by Mazo, which shows Velázquez in the background at his easel. Above, probably a copy of an original* Self-Portrait, *now lost (Florence, Pitti). Velázquez is shown wearing the key of a gentleman of the wardrobe on his belt.*

handled in the same luminous manner as is the naturalism and plasticity of Caravaggio's paintings. Instead these canvases, particularly in a certain hardness of outline, reflect the disciplined approach to drawing which he learned in Pacheco's studio, in marked contrast to the qualities characteristic of Caravaggio's paintings.

Recent studies have shown that even before 1618 a number of works by painters of the Andalusian and specifically Sevillian school displayed a naturalist or 'tenebrist' approach which had nothing to do with the naturalism of Caravaggio. Before Velázquez several Sevillian painters (Pablo Legote, Herrera the Elder) had already portrayed subjects and figures taken from popular life in their canvases, combining these with a still-life element. The compositional schemes which Velázquez adopted in his *bodegones* with figures (including those with religious scenes set in the background) are certainly derived from Flemish models popular all over southern Spain. Even his more strictly religious paintings (*The Immaculate Conception* (No. 4), *St John* (No. 3), *The Adoration of the Magi* (No. 7), *Christ at Emmaus* (No. 22)) owe nothing to Caravaggio but, like his early portraits, are most likely influenced by iconographic models typical of local tradition. In both the religious paintings and the portraits he painted during this period there is the same eager pursuit of the concrete as in his remarkable *bodegones*.

And so Velázquez' great achievement during his Sevillian period was his transformation of existing elements of the native Spanish tradition into something new and original. He acquired not only superior technical and artistic skills, but a deep sense of humanity, reflecting the extraordinary equilibrium, both mental and artistic, which he was to display throughout his life.

Velázquez' development of these qualities continued during his first visit to Madrid in spring 1622 and his move there in summer 1623. Residence in the capital meant not only a chance to satisfy his understandable ambition to become established in court circles (throughout his life he keenly pursued commissions at court); but above all the change of scene broadened his experience, releasing him from the more restricted artistic circles in his native Seville.

The canvas of *St Ildefonso receiving the Chasuble* (No. 26), dating from between 1622 and 1623, is an early attempt to extend the range of the works Velázquez painted in Seville before his first visit to Madrid. Here we find echoes of El Greco. There is also a softer handling of light inspired, according to some writers, by Caravaggio or, more probably, by the work of one of his followers, like Bartolomeo Cavarozzi who may have worked in Madrid.

Velázquez finally moved to Madrid on the invitation of Don Gaspar de Guzmán, Count of Olivares (soon to be better known as the count-duke), Philip IV's powerful chief minister and, like Velázquez, a native of Andalusia. After painting his first portrait of the king in August he was appointed court painter on 6 October 1623. These two events provided Velázquez, then still a young man, with stimulation to consider new problems. The appointment gave him an opportunity to become familiar with the rich art collections in the royal palace, in which he soon had the chance to take up residence with his family. Above all he could study the many paintings there by the great Venetian masters of the Cinquecento, especially Titian and Tintoretto. From these he must have gained precious insights into ways of resolving a series of problems – above all the relationship between light, form and colour – which had so exercised him during his early days in Seville. But his contact with the great works of the Venetian Cinquecento did not mean an immediate renunciation of the values of his earlier paintings. In the portraits of the king, the count-duke and other court figures, which date from before his visit to Italy in 1629, and particularly in the famous *Los Borrachos* (*Bacchus* or *The Topers* (No. 39)) of 1628, he still displays his original concern with capturing reality, whether he is painting the king or the coarser figures of the drinkers grouped round Bacchus. However, this now involves him in an analysis of sensory data, an exploration of shifting patterns of light, instead of the painstaking portrayal of minute detail characteristic of his early compositions. To return to the *Bacchus*: this painting shows that Velázquez might have gained certain insights into the main concerns of sixteenth-century Venetian painting from Rubens, who made his second visit to Madrid in August 1628 and with whom he was friendly. The work also harks back to the *bodegones* with figures of his Seville days. But the totally different atmosphere and new three-dimensional qualities of the images in this painting, compared with the more austere handling of volume in a work like *The Waterseller* (No. 17), in the Wellington Museum, must be due largely to the painter's new feeling for the use of warm colour and brilliant light, as shown in Titian's work.

The portrait of *Philip IV* in armour (No. 35), now in the Prado, also shows that Velázquez' familiarity with Venetian works in the royal collections was a determining factor, even before his visit to Italy, in his new feeling for light and his approach to reality. The portrait, probably begun in 1625, was completed in 1628 with the addition of the red scarf across the armour, an unexpected touch of colour which sets the dominant tone of the whole composition and clearly reflects aspects of Rubens' art. Compared with his earliest known portrait of the king (No. 27), now in the Meadows Museum, Dallas, painted a few years earlier and soon after the painter arrived in Madrid for the second time, the Prado portrait has obvious forerunners in Titian's portraits of Charles V and Philip II. Velázquez is no longer simply concerned with conveying the precise physical solidity and volume of his subject. His aim now is to capture with the same exactness qualities determined by the relationship between light, space and colour, atmospheric values which he now regards as of prime importance in his exploration of sensory experience and his vision, as a painter, of reality.

A voyage of study to Italy marked the culmination of his development during his early years at court, in the light of the new insights he gained from his familiarity with works in the royal collections and his friendship with Rubens. He left Spain in August 1629 and returned early in 1631 after visiting Genoa, Milan, Venice, Ferrara, Cento, Bologna, Loreto, Rome and Naples (where he met Ribera and painted a portrait of the Infanta Maria, Philip IV's sister, then on her way to Hungary to marry Ferdinand III). His

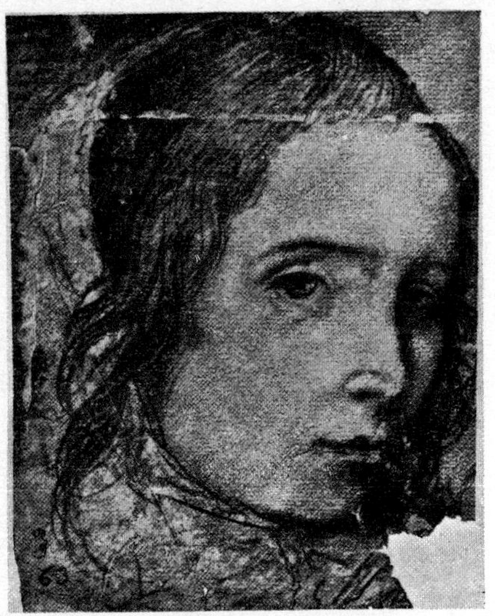

It has been suggested that this Young Girl *(Madrid, Biblioteca Nacional) may be Velázquez' wife, though there is no evidence for this.*

stay in Italy, especially his visits to Venice, Rome and Naples, helped to strengthen perceptions which had come to him as he studied canvases by Titian and Tintoretto in Madrid, rather than marking any dramatic change in direction. It completed the maturing process begun years before in Pacheco's workshop by allowing him to clarify and deepen the highly personal view of painting already apparent in works he painted in Madrid just before his journey to Italy, but only fully realized after 1630.

To be there, in the land of the great masters of the Italian Cinquecento, meant a chance to compare the different tendencies which existed in Italian painting, past and present, from Michelangelo to the Carracci, from Titian to Reni. Velázquez could test his new attraction towards Venetian painting and see whether here he might find what he had been seeking: a form of painting which could express reality not just by conveying material being, or a distorted or idealized version of it, but by translating into painting – into form and colour – the emotions created by reality itself. This was the only way, not to produce 'realistic' painting, but to make painting itself real, an integral part of the experience of reality. It was also the great undertaking, as revolutionary and modern as Caravaggio's achievements years before, on which Velázquez embarked after his first visit to Italy and which makes his painting a vital and artistic experience that is still acutely relevant today.

During this first visit to Italy Velázquez had occasion to express his conception of the relationship between painting and reality by tackling one of the commonest and most fruitful themes of the Italian tradition–the classical heritage, as expressed in terms of pagan and Christian mythology. *The Forge of Vulcan* (No. 43) and *Joseph's Bloody Coat brought to Jacob* (No. 41), the two most famous canvases painted during his stay in Italy (in fact, while in Rome), are fine examples. Here we see the painter fascinated by his discovery of the values inherent in the art and culture of antiquity, especially as expressed in the plastic beauty of the nude. Yet for all the charm that the classical held for Velázquez he avoided the pitfall of mythologizing. The living beauty of his young nudes, depicted with almost academic perfection and purely aesthetic delight, is totally free of intellectualizing. There is no attempt to express an abstract ideal of beauty in painting. Instead we find an intense feeling for the beauty of living forms exactly translated into pictorial terms.

Velázquez returned to Madrid where for almost twenty years he continued his steady rise to the highest offices open to a court artist. He became court usher in late 1633, gentleman of the wardrobe the following year, gentleman of the bedchamber and assistant superintendent of works in 1643 and in 1646 gentleman of the bed chamber 'with duties'. He concentrated most of his energies on perfecting the artistic tools he had acquired from his earlier and recent study of the Venetian Cinquecento painters, his aim still being to explore visual reality through an examination of the relationships between light, space and colour.

This undertaking occupied him until his second visit to Italy, and he was to return to it with fresh awareness and a greater sense of freedom in his last works. The results can be seen in his marvellous series of portraits of members of the royal family and court figures, and in a number of equally fine paintings on a range of subjects – religious (*St Anthony Abbot and St Paul the Hermit* (No. 87), *The Coronation of the Virgin* (No. 93); secular (*Head of a Stag* (No. 70), *Menippus* (No. 83), *Aesop* (No. 84); historical (*The Surrender of Breda* (No. 65); and mythological (*Mars* (No. 85), *Venus at her Mirror* (No. 106)).

In these paintings Velázquez abandoned once and for all his youthful preoccupation with the almost tangible portrayal of three-dimensional form and his predominant use of impasto. With increasing sureness of touch he now preferred fluid, vibrant brushwork, allowing a skilful build-up of masses of colour, highlighted by silvery tones to create a feeling of brilliance and light. He successfully expressed in his painting the most concrete results of his investigation of and deep feelings for the real world, feelings which acquired new meaning and permanence as he translated them into pictorial experience. This meant a heightening of the visual qualities of light, colour and space which alone gave appearances substance and allowed the innermost secrets of the human heart to find concrete expression.

This approach produced some intensely powerful works: the light-filled landscape of *St Anthony Abbot and St Paul the Hermit* (No. 87); the famous *Surrender of Breda* (No. 65), a complex and consciously exploratory work which – with the seeming simplicity of its compositional patterns, the painter's scrupulous attention to formal elements and detail, and the shimmering effects of light – hints at some of the solutions later to appear in more highly developed form in *Las Meninas* (*The Maids of Honour*) (No. 123) or *Las Hilanderas* (*The Fable of Arachne*, (No. 126)); the touching *Venus at her Mirror* (No. 106), in which the beauty of the subject is heightened by the telling use of colour offset by silvery tones and cooler hues.

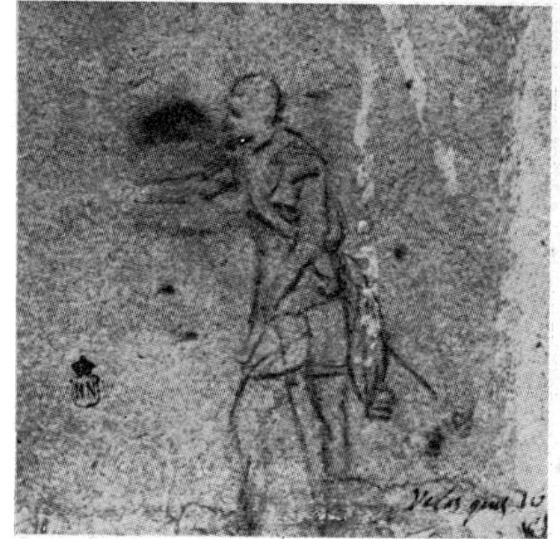

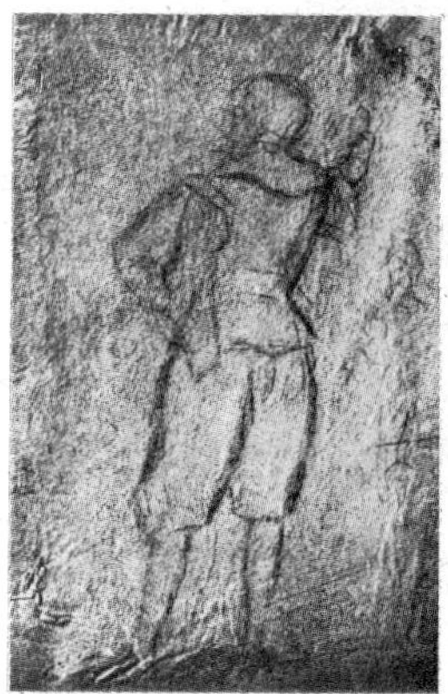

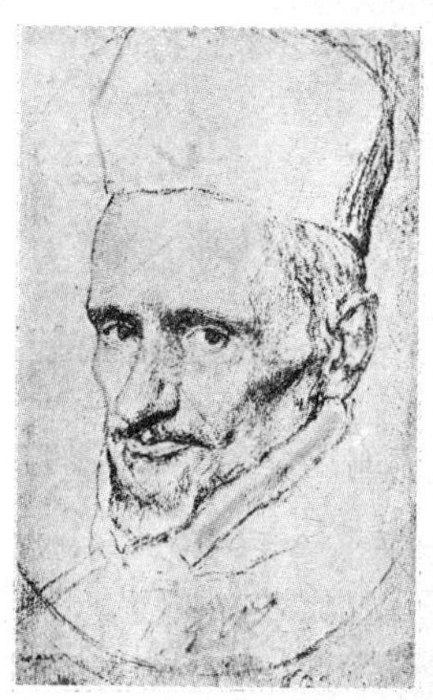

Drawings by Velázquez. Top and centre (Madrid, Biblioteca Nacional), studies for The Surrender of Breda *(No. 65). Bottom (Madrid, Real Academia de San Fernando), study for the portrait of* Cardinal Borgia *(No. 96).*

But Velázquez' modern conception of his art, matured after his first visit to Italy, reached its height in the large number of portraits commissioned during this period. In these images, usually of individual figures in hunting clothes or on horseback set against a real landscape bathed in brilliant light, his penetrating understanding of human nature and the world found apt expression.

On cursory inspection this extraordinary succession of kings and princesses, artists and ministers, cardinals, court jesters and dwarfs seems to reveal nothing of the painter's remarkable capacity, so often mentioned by scholars, for entering fully into the condition of other men, a gift seen in the works of his Seville period and his early years in Madrid. Can Velázquez really be as detached, as seemingly indifferent to the contrasting conditions of these extraordinary models of humanity as his portraits of elegant princes and stunted clowns suggest? Can these proud portraits of king and courtiers really not reflect anything of the dramatic changes of fortune which at this time were pushing Spain towards the brink of political and economic collapse and her final decline as a great European power?

A closer examination of the artist's mature works cannot ignore the conditions imposed on him, particularly in his formal official portraits, by state patronage and its demand for ceremonial works. The impartiality of his approach to the king's elegant figure or a court jester's stunted form, the apparent imperturbability of his subjects in the face of changing fortune and decline, seem an expression of the impassive, even phlegmatic side of his temperament, commented on by all his biographers, and obviously the result of an untroubled and prosperous life spent almost entirely under court protection. Yet these qualities in fact reflect his determination to explore the innermost nature of men and things, and his firm belief that only in this way could he understand and overcome the limitations and incidentals of the real world. Only painting, or the work of the painter, offered a tool for overcoming those aspects of reality which he felt to be ephemeral, irrelevant, distressing or restricting.

Velázquez developed his essential ideas about his art during the years following his first visit to Italy. His surprisingly modern view of the relationship between painting and reality did not, if properly understood, mark a rejection of his youthful approach, but was rather the outcome of a profound experience of artistic growth and developing awareness. It did not change substantially with his second visit to Italy from January 1649 to June 1651.

During this second visit Velázquez' main ports of call were Venice, Naples and Rome. In Rome in spring 1650 he painted one of his most famous and powerful works, the portrait of *Innocent X* (No. 113) in the Galleria Doria Pamphili, and was admitted into the Academy of the 'Virtuosi al Pantheon' and the Academy of Saint Luke. Unlike his earlier visit, this one was not devoted to study or to extending his knowledge of Italian art. Philip IV had himself asked Velázquez to make the journey in order to acquire antique statues and paintings mainly of the Venetian school. At fifty Velázquez' artistic experience was so rich and varied, his conception of painting so advanced, that he probably felt little need to bring himself up to date on new developments in Italian art over the last twenty years.

Nonetheless the visit did make an impact on his later work. He returned to the Venetian canvases he had first studied twenty years before with a far more mature understanding, in the light of what he had been trying to do in his own work over recent years. This reappraisal not only convinced him that his approach had been valid, but also suggested to him ways of extending the means of expression in painting which he had been using to such good effect. As his powers of perception and his ability to probe innermost reality grew over the years, his conviction that painting was the only possible concrete expression of reality, and indeed was itself reality, led him to a logical conclusion: the different elements of the painter's work must undergo a process of continual renewal and improvement. This may have been one reason he so often returned to retouch and alter works finished years before.

Velázquez' output after his return to Madrid seems, in many ways, a continuation of his earlier work. Appointed palace marshal by the king in February 1652 and created a knight of Santiago in 1658 after various bureaucratic hindrances, he produced a series of portraits of members of the royal family, including the famous *Maids of Honour* (No. 123), breaking off only for two paintings of mythological subjects, *The Fable of Arachne* (No. 126) and *Mercury and Argus* (No. 127). The problem of the relationship between light, space and colour is the same in *The Maids of Honour* (No. 123) as in *The Surrender of Breda* (No. 65). The later portraits of the king, the Infanta Margarita and Prince Felipe Próspero posed the same problems of composition as those of the king, queen and infantes painted between his two visits to Italy.

Yet in the later works the painter chose quite different solutions to these problems. The brush strokes are broader and even more fluid, but at the same time more sure, almost geometrically exact. The chromatic solutions which Velázquez adopted have led scholars to remark on his use of dissociated 'blobs' of colour. Forms are dissolved, hard outlines melt away, matter seems to quiver with life in the light-filled air which so tangibly separates figures and objects. All this has suggested a direct connection between Velázquez' late work and French Impressionism, a documented link in the case of some of Manet's paintings.

In these last works it is light, real and all-pervasive, which creates the sense of air, as something actually there, as an element which can modify the appearance of reality. Light also determines the consistency of space in these paintings, here essentially pictorial since always resulting from the skilful use and juxtaposition of colour, different textures and qualities reacting in different ways to the dominant effect of light. This again was a revolutionary concept which Velázquez passed on to future generations of artists from the Impressionists to Picasso.

Velázquez fell ill in July 1660, worn out by his exertions in preparing the royal quarters in Fuenterrabia on the Isle of Pheasants, where Philip IV was to give his daughter Maria Teresa in marriage to Louis XIV of France. He died in Madrid on 6 August that year.

***St John writing the Apocalypse* (*No. 3, detail*).**
It is generally agreed that this dates from 1618–19, though not everyone accepts Allende-Salazar's suggestion that the saint is a self-portrait. The painting is one of the most important examples of Velázquez' naturalism during his early years in Seville and in many respects parallels Zurbarán's style.

Catalogue of the Paintings

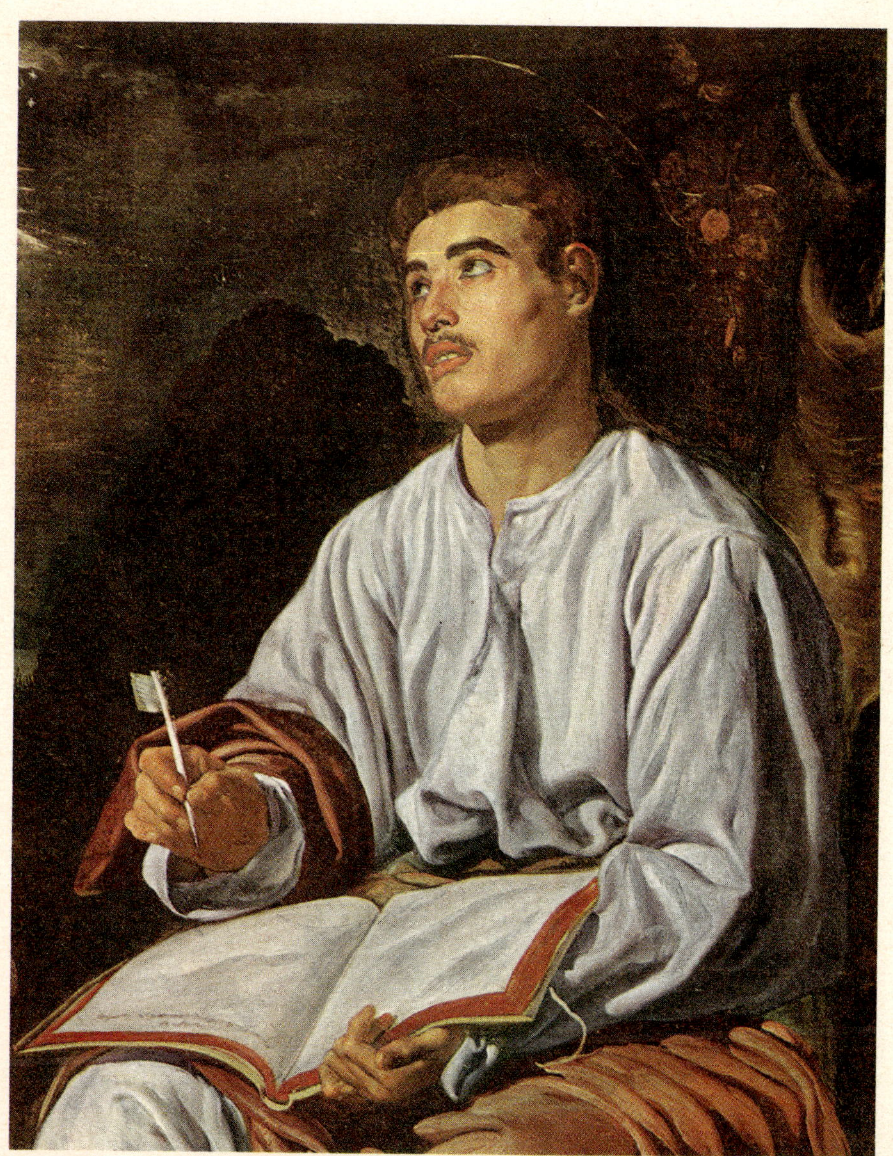

All measurements are in centimetres
s.d. = signed and dated
** denotes paintings about which there is any doubt at all as to attribution*

1 The Vintager
Oil on canvas/72 × 104/1617
New York, Cintas Collection

2 Musical Trio
Oil on canvas/87 × 110/1617–18
Berlin, Staatliche Museen

3 St John writing the Apocalypse
Oil on canvas/135 × 102/1618–19
London, National Gallery

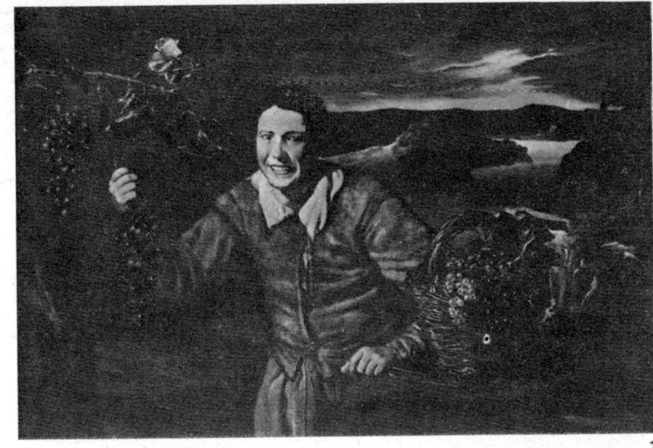
1

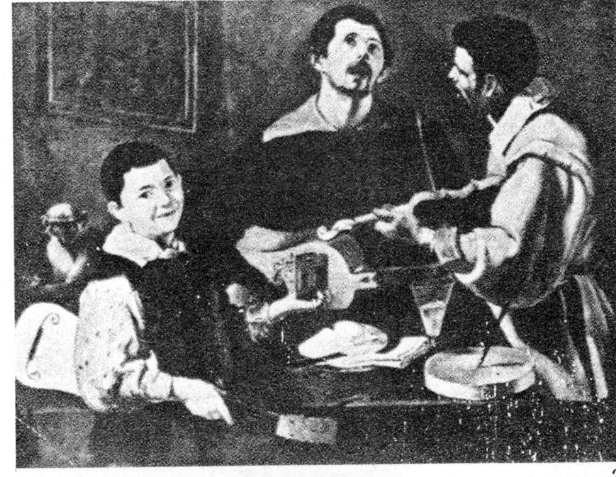
2

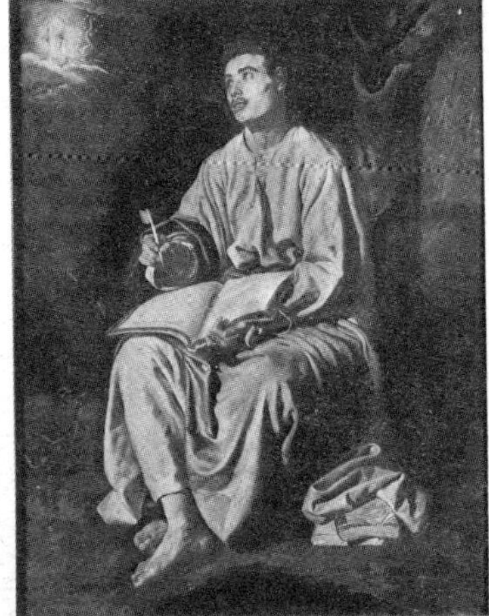
3

***The Adoration of the Magi* (*No. 7*)**
The work still displays many features typical of Velázquez' early naturalism in Seville including the choice of models. It is brighter in tonality than other works of the same period, thanks to a more cautious use of bitumen. The very simple and straight-forward compositional scheme is totally conventional, reminiscent of works by Tristán and Luís de Vargas.

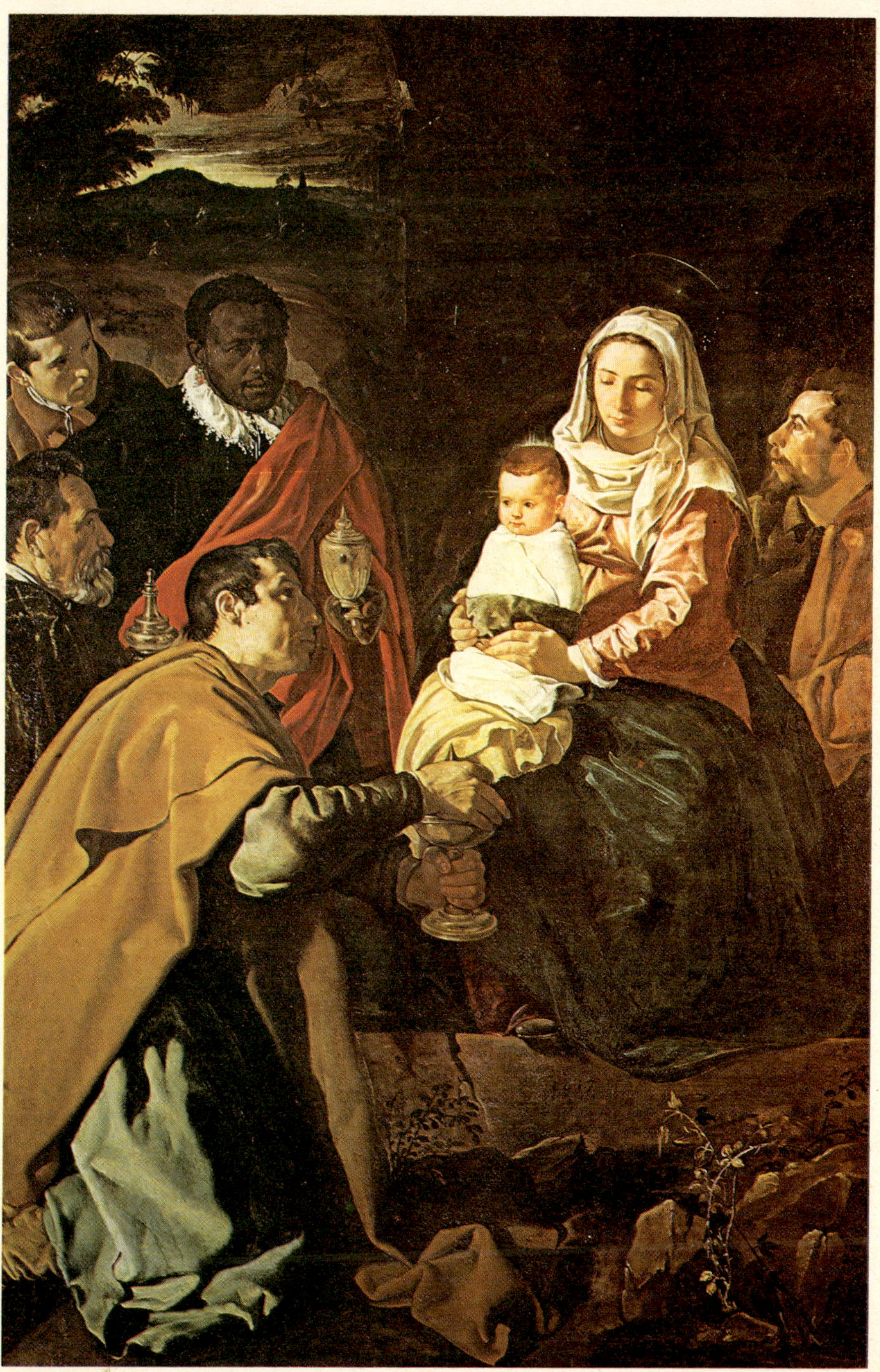

***Old Woman frying Eggs* (*No. 12*)**

One of the best known of Velázquez' early works. The painting owes less to Caravaggio than to works in a similar vein by Sevillian artists. It also shows the influence of Flemish models which Velázquez probably also knew from prints and engravings.

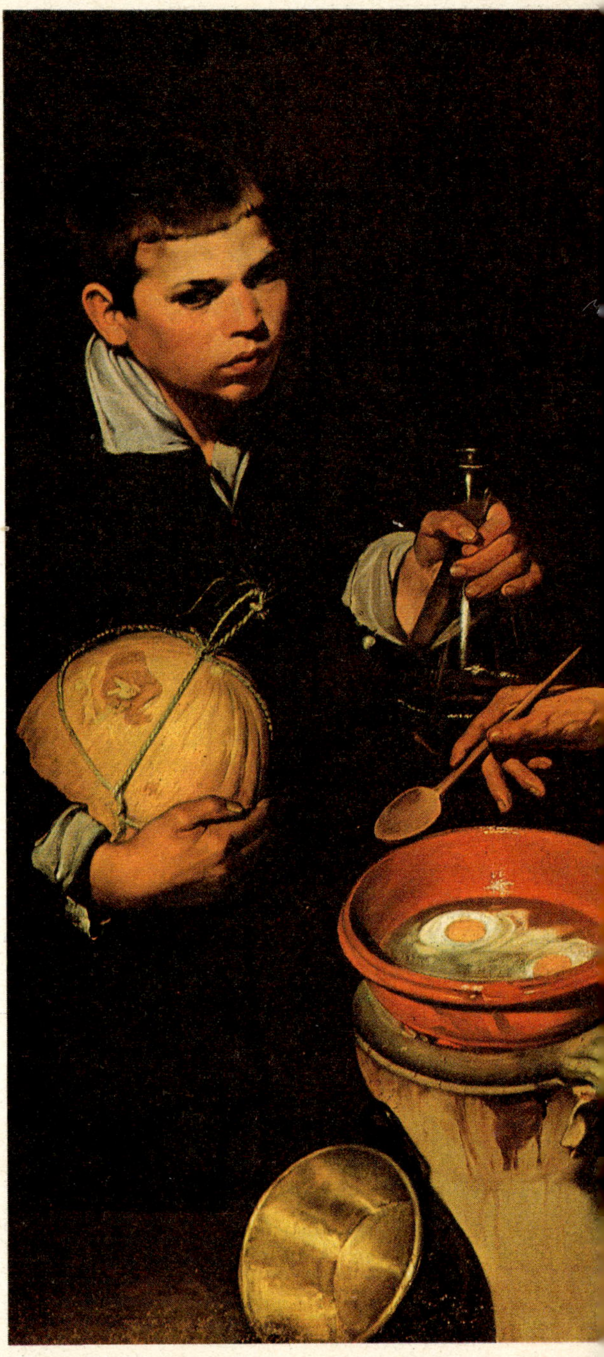

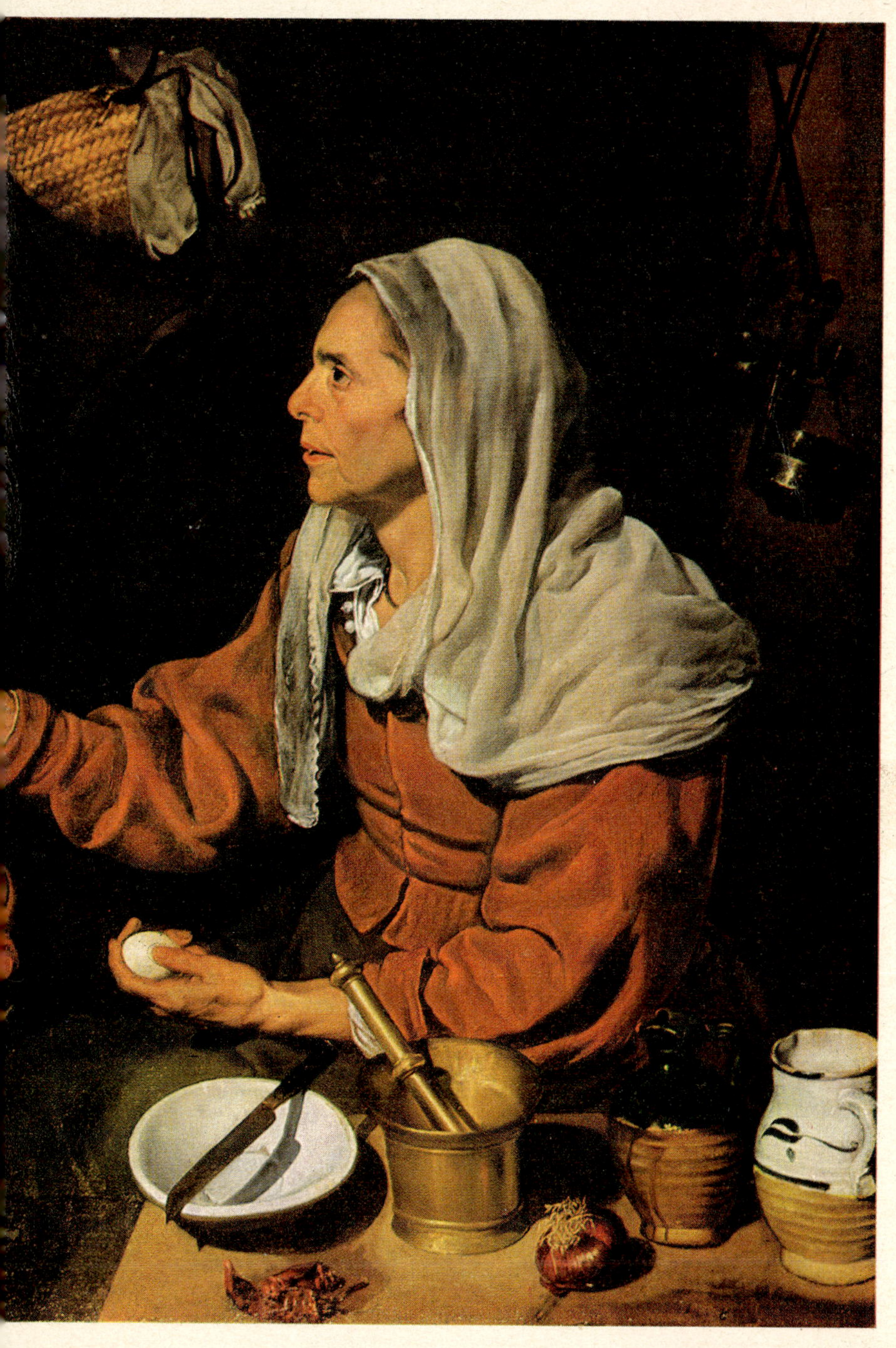

4 The Immaculate Conception
Oil on canvas/135 × 102/
1618–19
London, National Gallery

5 A Young Man
Oil on canvas/39 × 36/
1618–19
Leningrad, Hermitage

6 A Girl and Two Men at Table
Oil on canvas/96 × 112/
1618–19
Budapest, Szépmüvészeti Múzeum

7 The Adoration of the Magi
Oil on canvas/203 × 125/
1619 (?)
Madrid, Prado

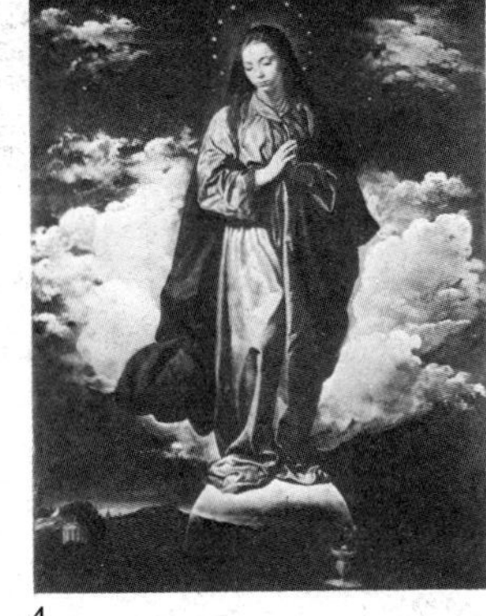

4

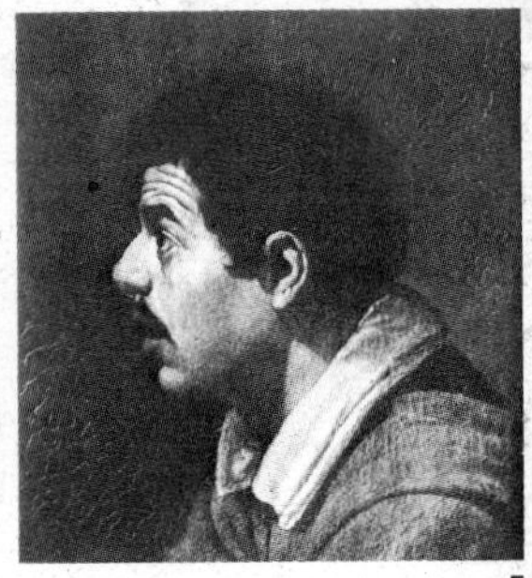

5

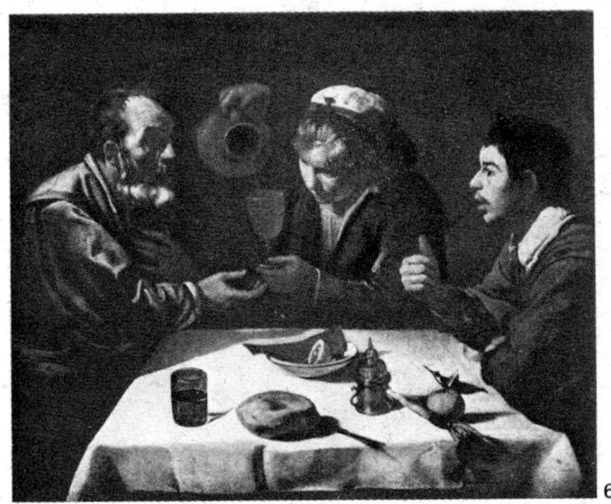

6

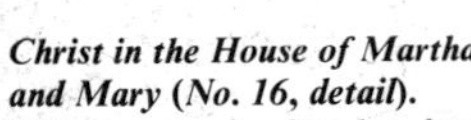

***Christ in the House of Martha and Mary* (*No. 16, detail*).**
This canvas, closely related to other bodegones *by Velázquez from about this time, includes the old woman (shown in this detail), who also appears in the* Old Woman frying Eggs. *The iconography, horizontal format and insertion of the religious episode in the background, as if seen through a small window, link the work to a series of Flemish paintings of similar subjects dating from the end of the sixteenth and beginning of the seventeenth centuries; there were then a number of these in Seville and others were known from engravings.*

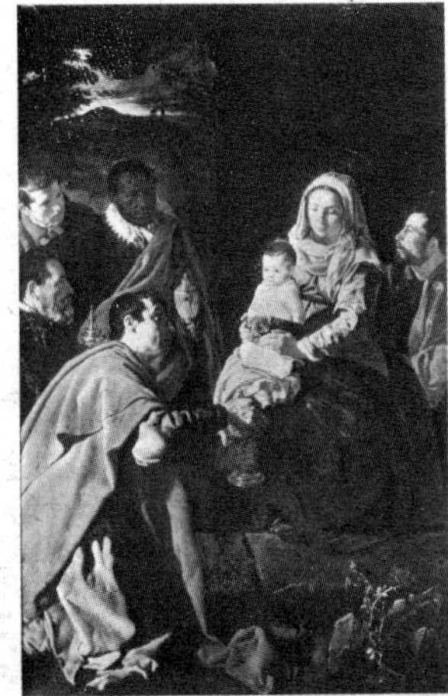

7

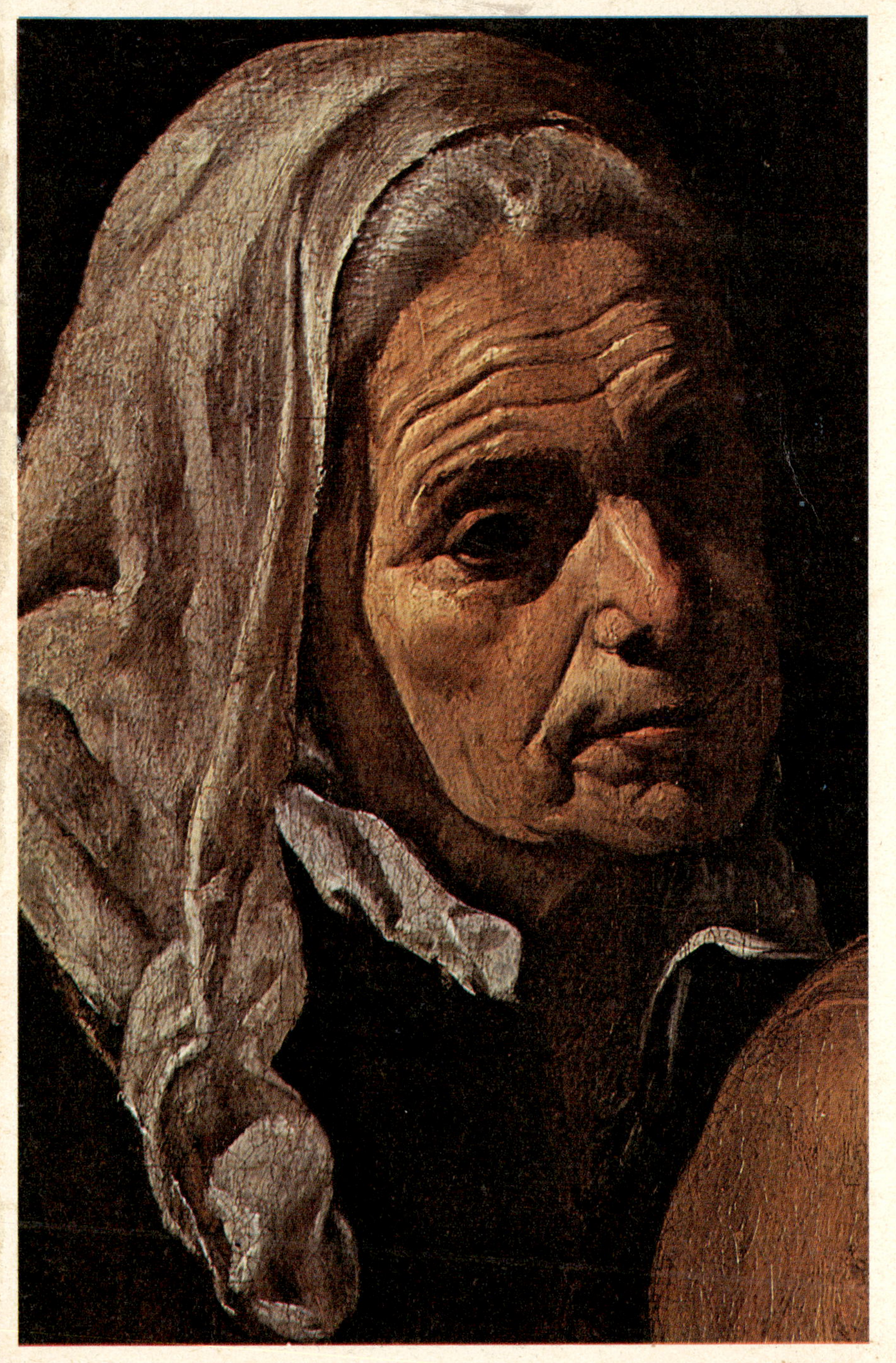

8 Three Men at Table
Oil on canvas/107 × 101/
1617–20
Leningrad, Hermitage

9 Two Young Men at Table
Oil on canvas/64.5 × 105/
1618–20
London, Wellington Museum

10 Christ at Emmaus
Oil on canvas/55 × 118/
1618–20
Blessington (Dublin), Beit Collection

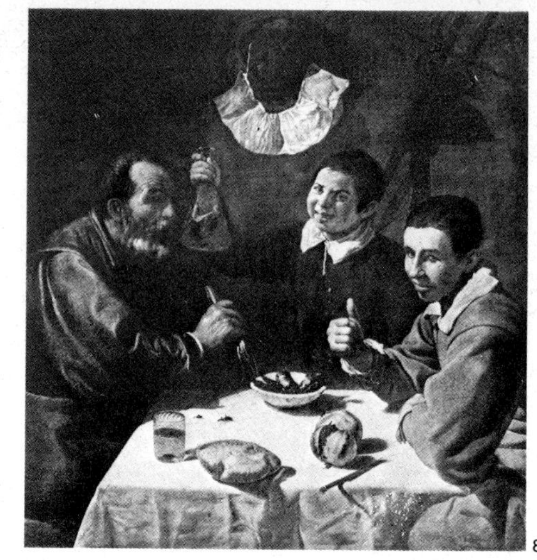

8

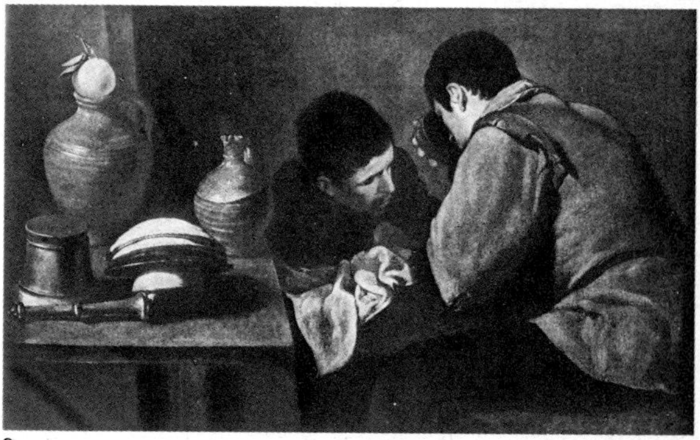

9

The Waterseller (No. 17). *Generally regarded as the finest work of Velázquez' Sevillian period, and perhaps the best support for the unproven hypothesis that he was familiar with works by the great naturalist Caravaggio and his early Roman followers. However, the particular interest of this work lies in the humanity of the artist's approach to his subject, seen in one simple but effective detail – the hands touching as the old man gives the glass to the boy.*

10

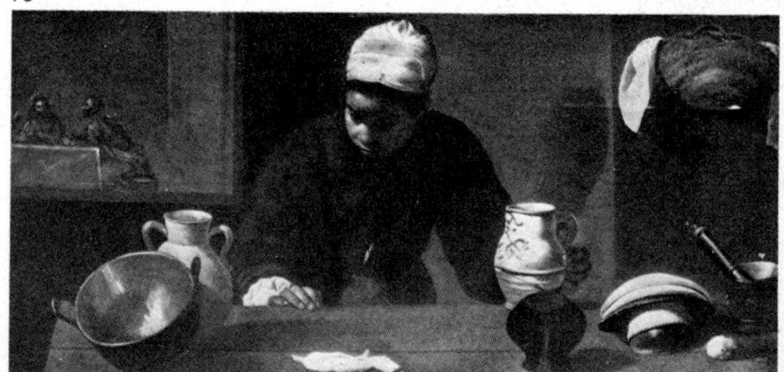

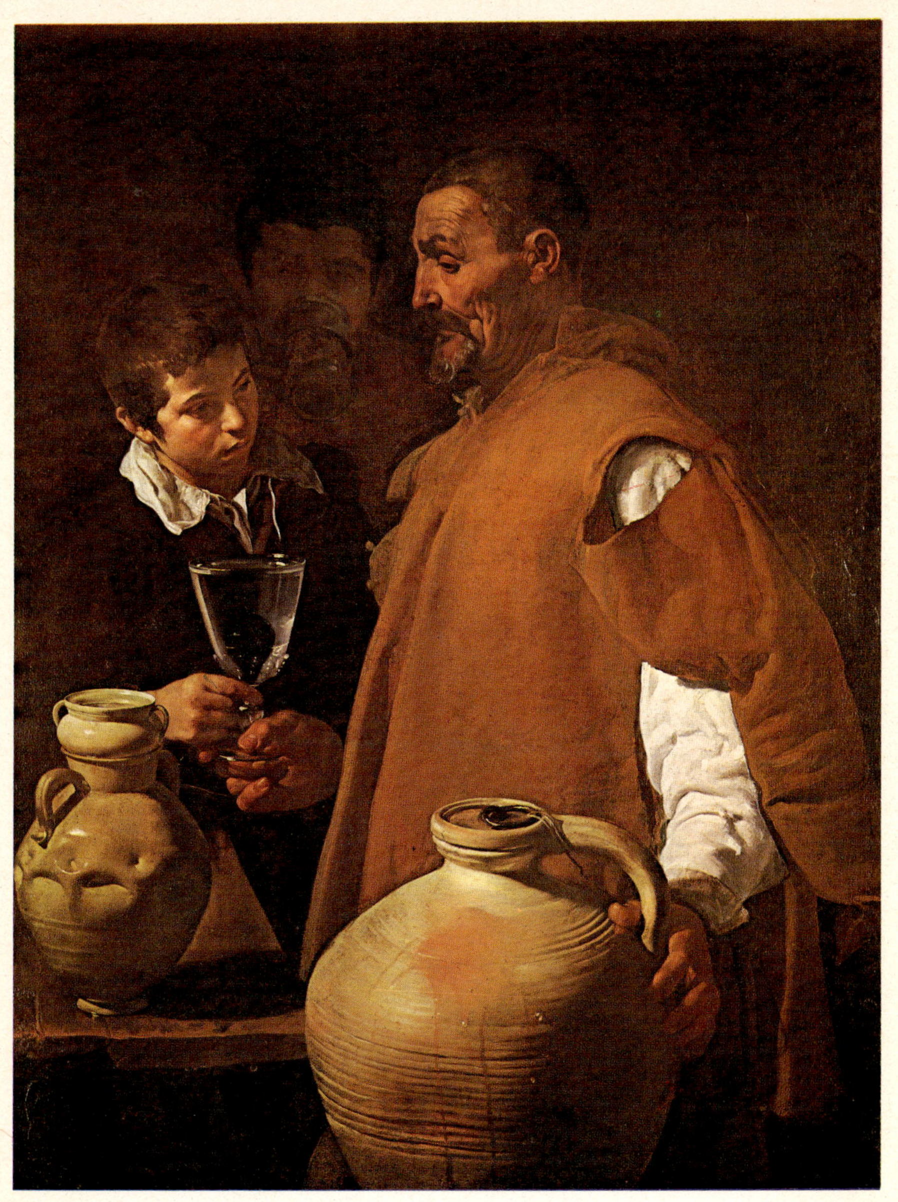

11 The Servant
Oil on canvas/55.7 × 104.5/
1618–20
Chicago, Art Institute

12 Old Woman frying Eggs
Oil on canvas/99 × 128/
1618–20
Edinburgh, National Gallery
of Scotland

13 St Paul
Oil on canvas/99 × 78/
1619–20
Barcelona, Museo de Arte de
Cataluña

14 St Paul
Oil on canvas/38 × 29/
1619–20
Madrid, Condesa de Saltes
Collection
Fragment

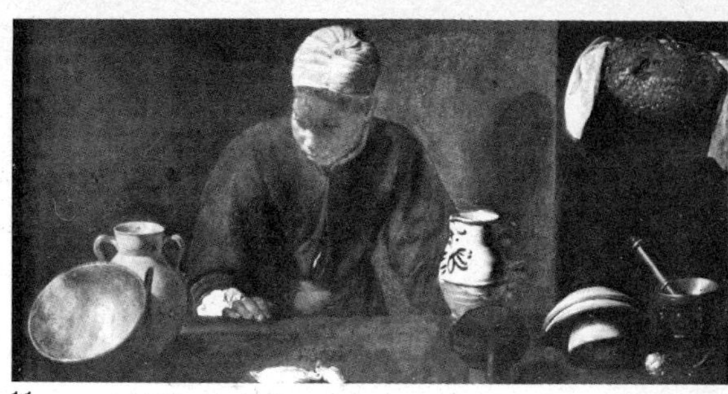

11

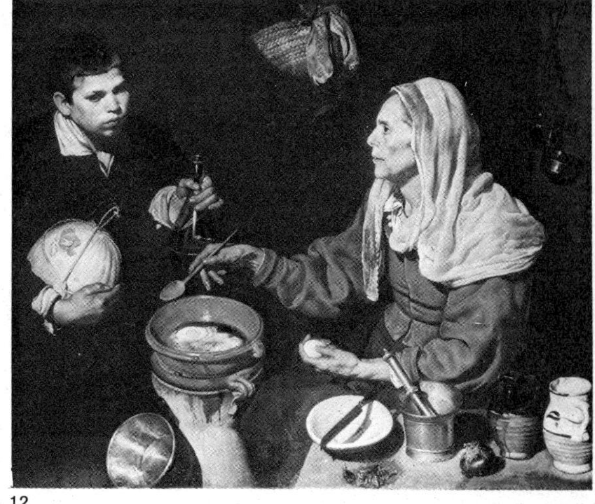

12

13

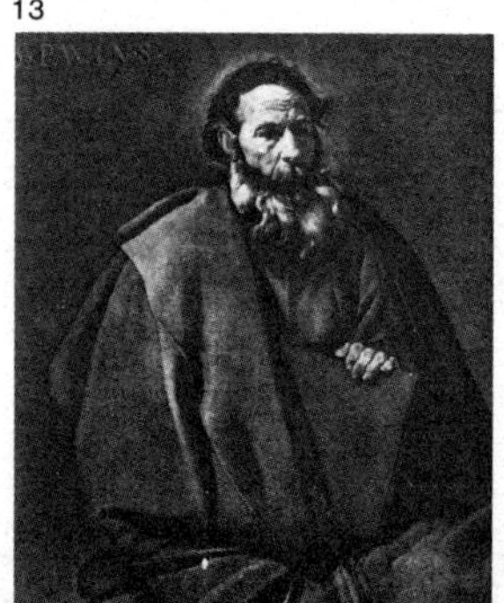

14

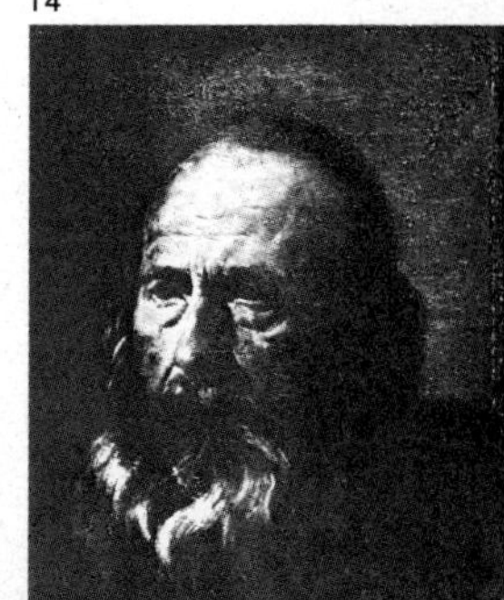

***Christ at Emmaus* (*No. 22, detail*).**
The canvas shows marked resemblances to works by Zurbarán and Herrera the Elder. What is new is the artist's use of light of almost supernatural intensity, not just as a compositional device, but to unite the figures of Christ and the two pilgrims and the objects on the dazzling white cloth.

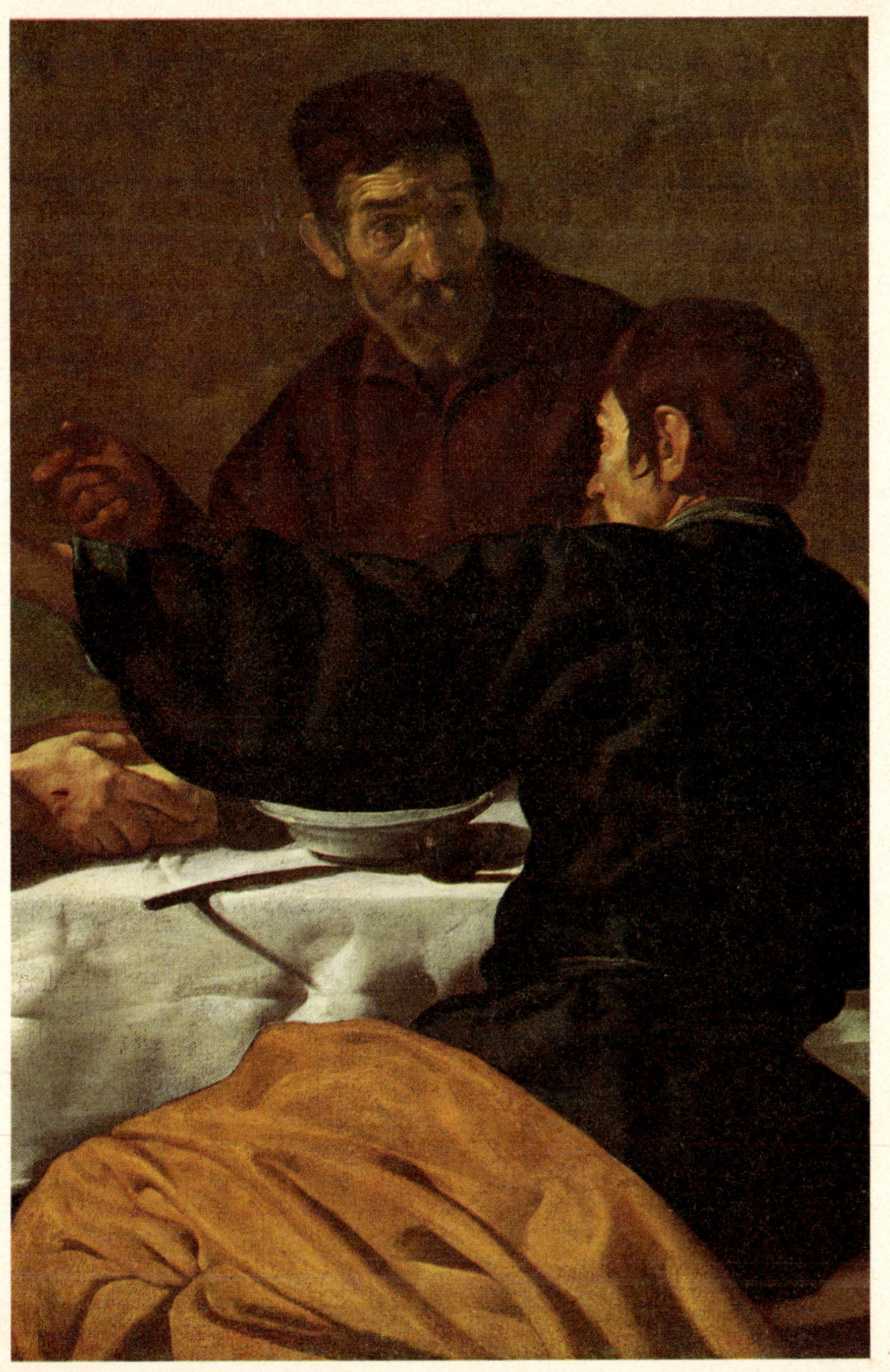

15 St Thomas
Oil on canvas/94 × 73/
1619–20
Orléans, Musée des Beaux-Arts

16 Christ in the House of Martha and Mary
Oil on canvas/60 × 103.5/
1619–20
London, National Gallery

17 The Waterseller
Oil on canvas/106 × 82/
1619–20
London, Wellington Museum

18 Cristóbal Suárez de Ribera
Oil on canvas/197 × 137/
s.d. 1620
Seville, Museo Provincial de Bellas Artes

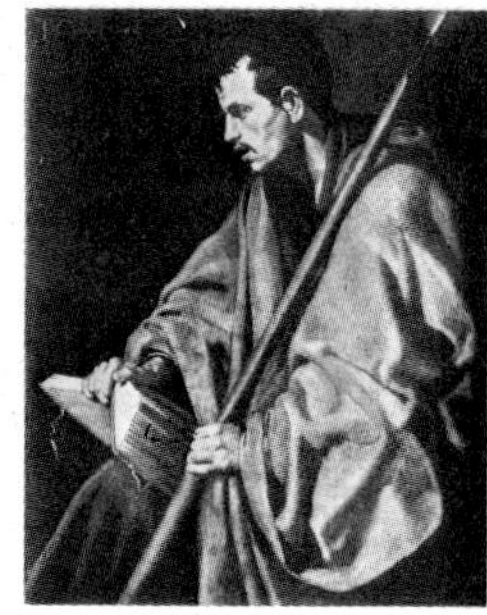

15

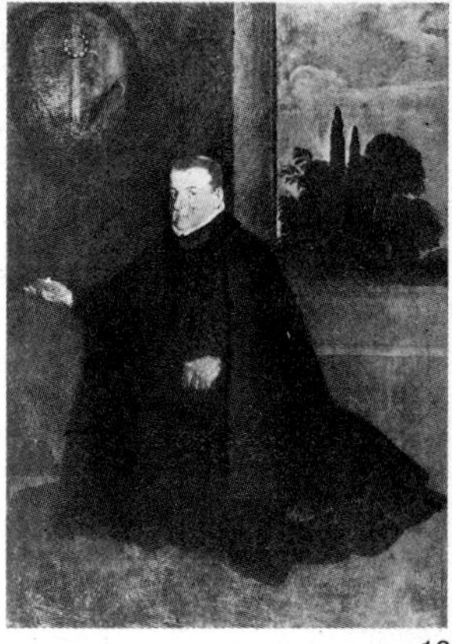

18

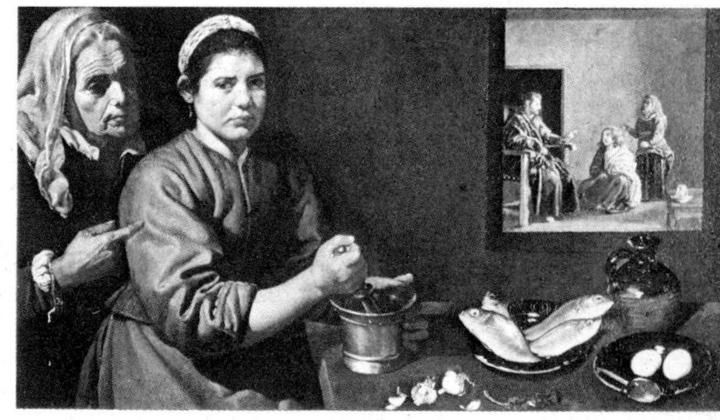

16

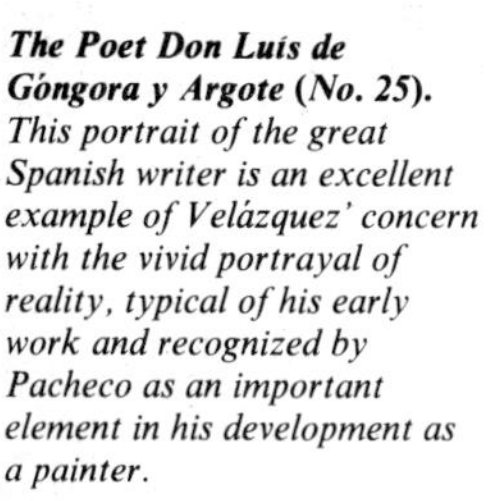

***The Poet Don Luís de Góngora y Argote* (*No. 25*).** *This portrait of the great Spanish writer is an excellent example of Velázquez' concern with the vivid portrayal of reality, typical of his early work and recognized by Pacheco as an important element in his development as a painter.*

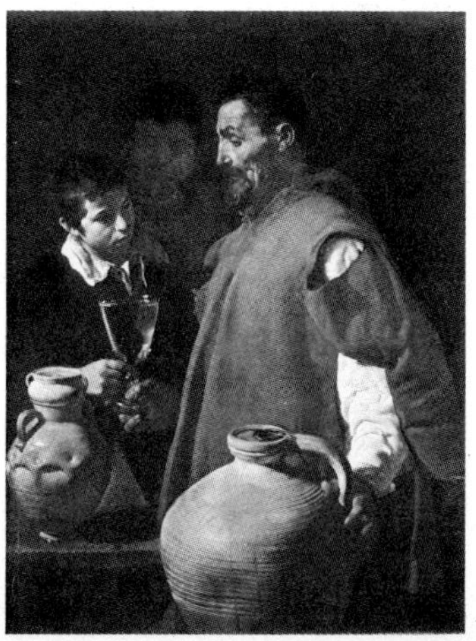

17

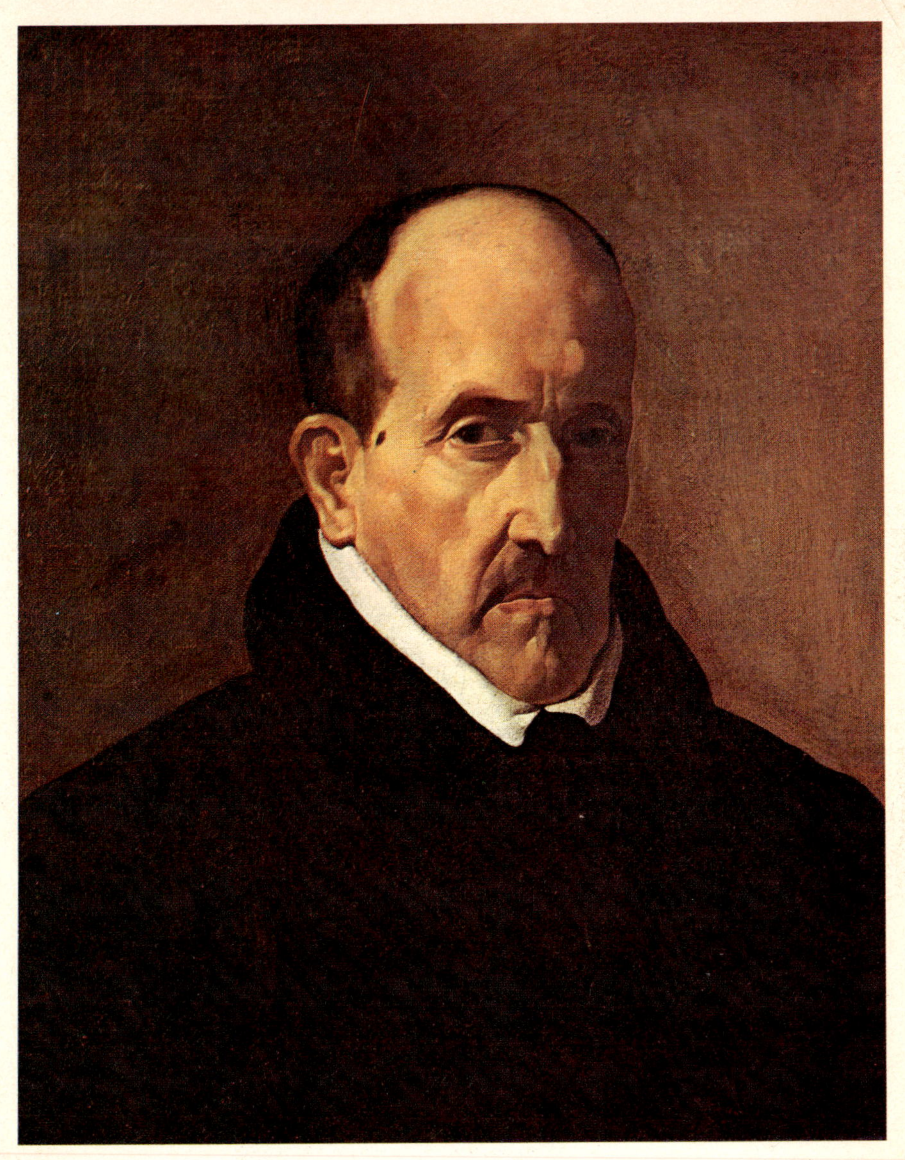

19 Doña Jerónima de la Fuente
Oil on canvas/160 × 110/ s.d. 1620
Madrid, Prado

20 Doña Jerónima de la Fuente
Oil on canvas/160 × 106/ s. 1620
Madrid, Fernández de Araóz Collection

21 Portrait of a Man with a Goatee (Francisco Pacheco (?))
Oil on canvas/40 × 36/1620
Madrid, Prado

22 Christ at Emmaus
Oil on canvas/123 × 132.6/ 1620
New York, Metropolitan Museum of Art

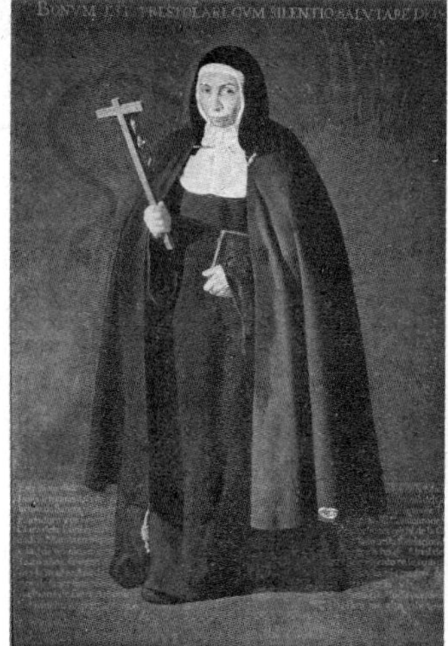

19

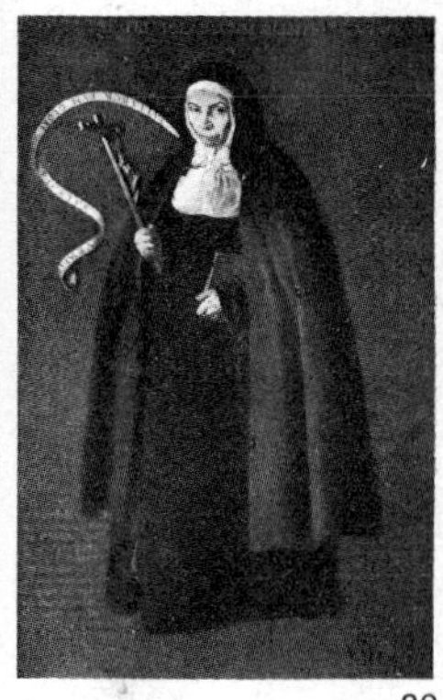

20

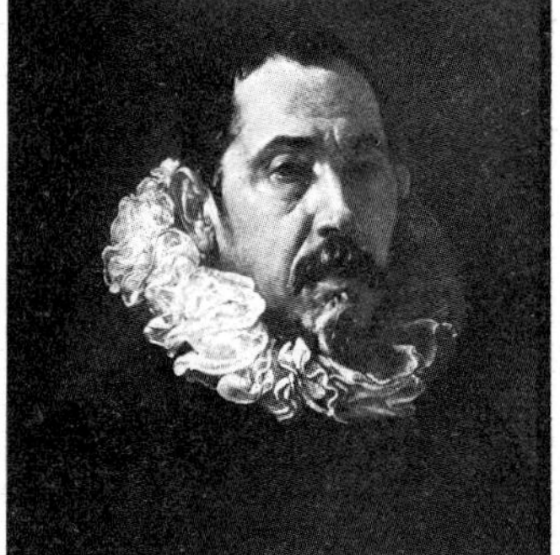

21

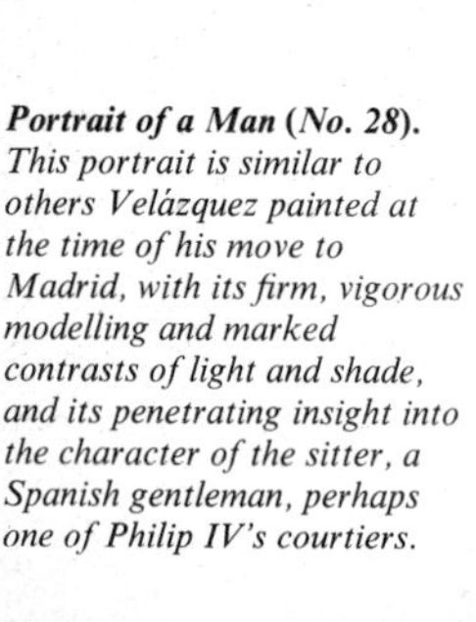

Portrait of a Man (No. 28). *This portrait is similar to others Velázquez painted at the time of his move to Madrid, with its firm, vigorous modelling and marked contrasts of light and shade, and its penetrating insight into the character of the sitter, a Spanish gentleman, perhaps one of Philip IV's courtiers.*

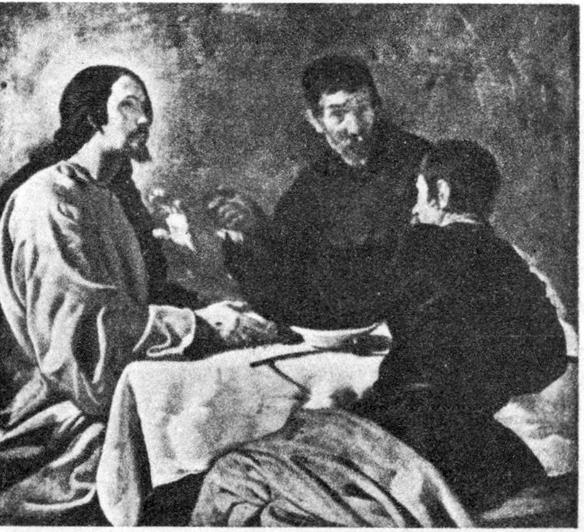

22

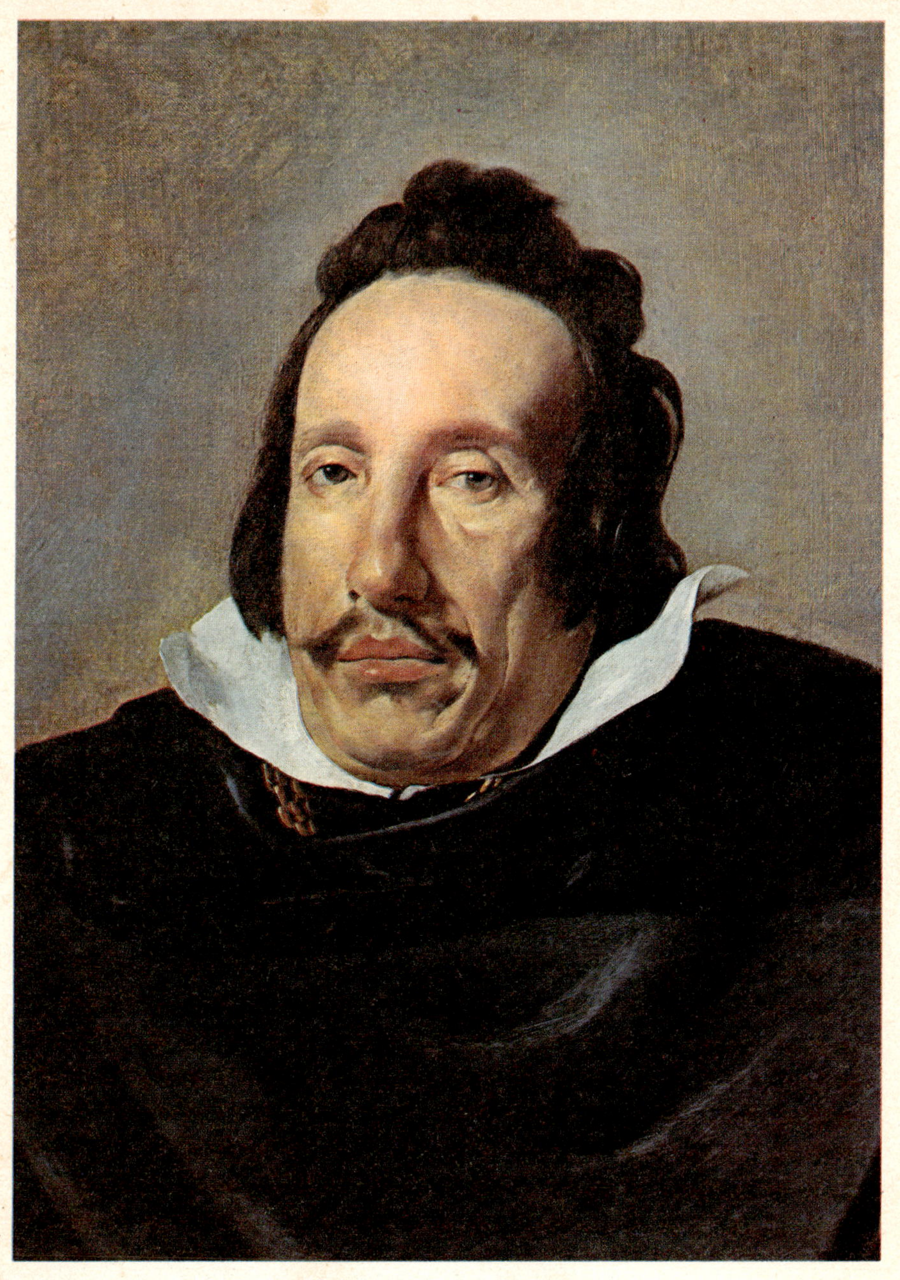

23 St John the Baptist*
Oil on canvas/175.3 × 152.5/1620
Chicago, Art Institute

24 Portrait of a Young Man (Self-portrait (?))
Oil on canvas/56 × 39/1620–22
Madrid, Prado

25 The Poet Don Luis de Góngora y Argote
Oil on canvas/51 × 41/1622
Boston, Museum of Fine Arts

26 St Ildefonso receiving the Chasuble
Oil on canvas/165 × 115/1623
Seville, Museo Provincial de Bellas Artes

Gaspar de Guzmán, Conde Duque de Olivares (No. 31, detail).
Velázquez had already painted another full-length portrait of Olivares in 1624 (No. 30, now in São Paulo, Brazil). Like that fine example of 'human architecture', this New York portrait (1625) is outstanding for the sternly monumental quality of the figure, posed deliberately to create compositional balance in a space economically indicated by the sparsely furnished room.

Bacchus ('Los Borrachos', No. 39. (pp. 28–9)
One of Velázquez' earliest paintings of a group of figures, and his last major work before the first trip to Italy. He treats his mythological subject as a pretext for an assortment of real-life Castillian peasants. Part of a carefully worked-out compositional scheme obviously influenced by Cinquecento models, they are portrayed with the lively naturalism of his early Sevillian works, in marked contrast to the beautiful Renaissance forms of Bacchus and the follower on his left.

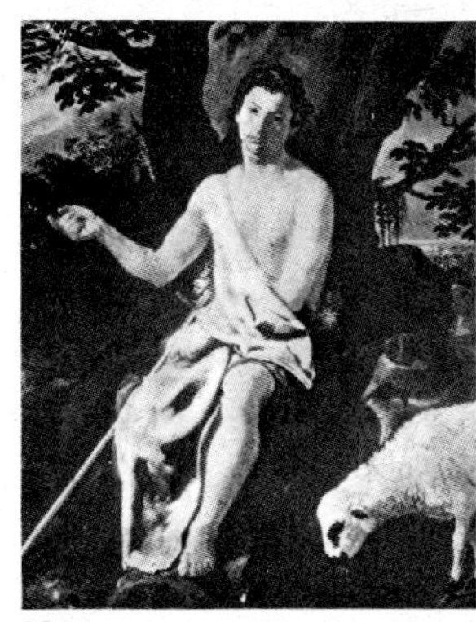
23

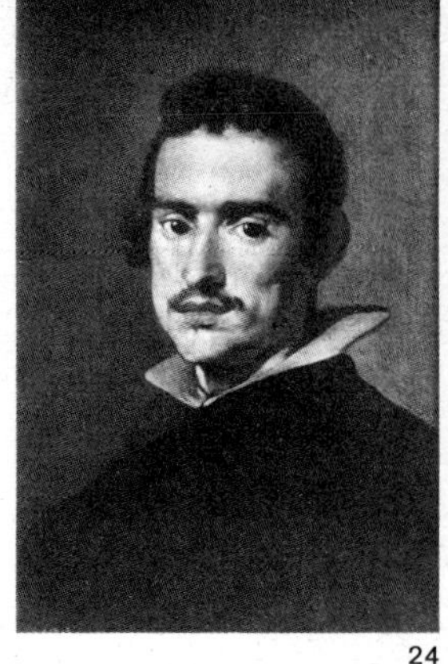
24

25

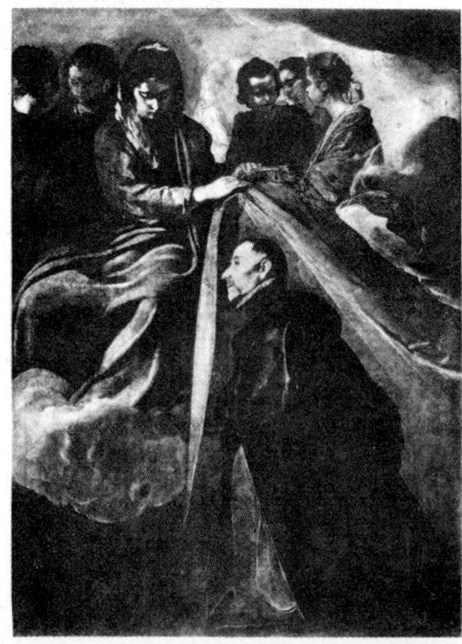
26

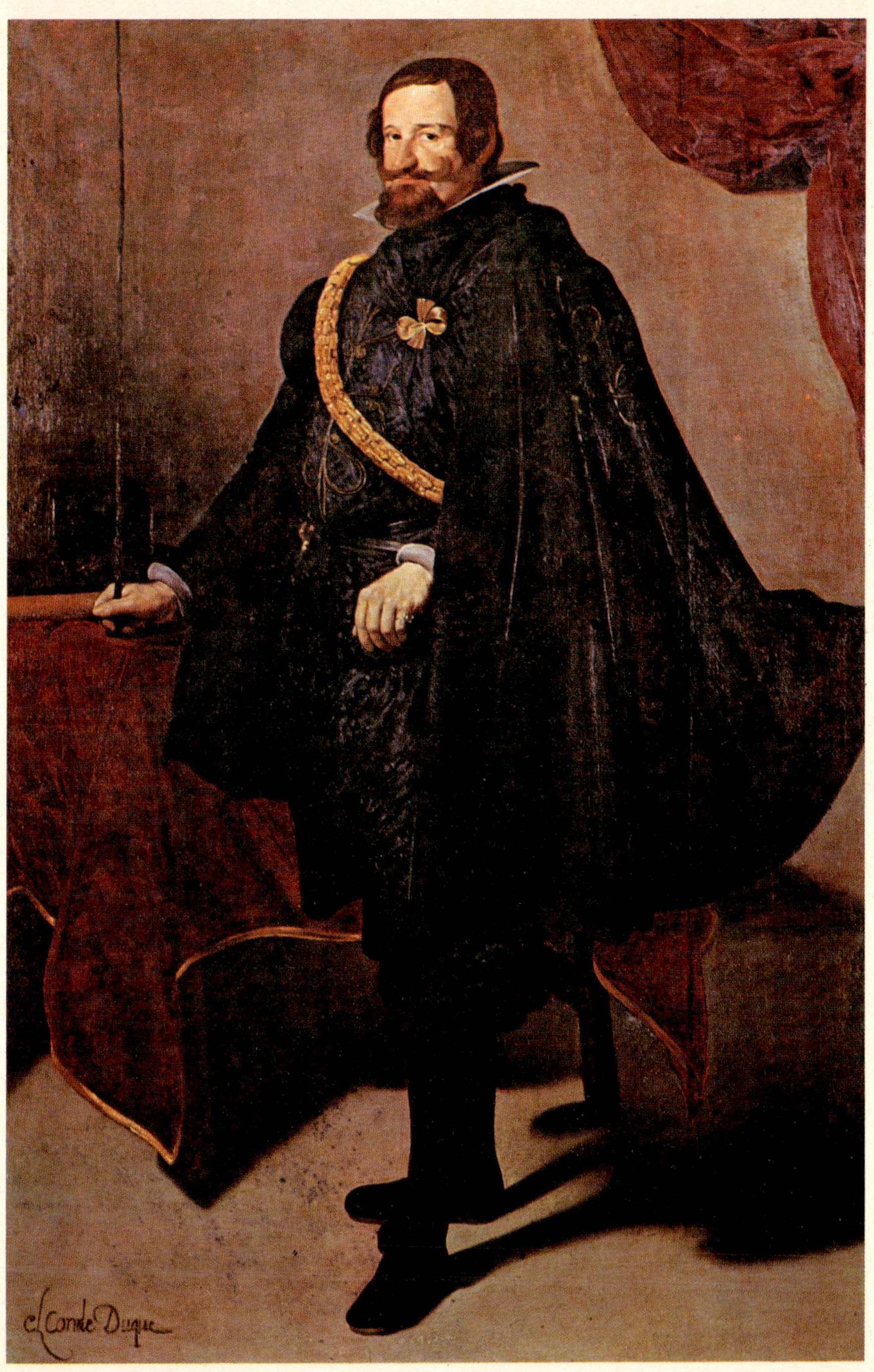
el Conde Duque

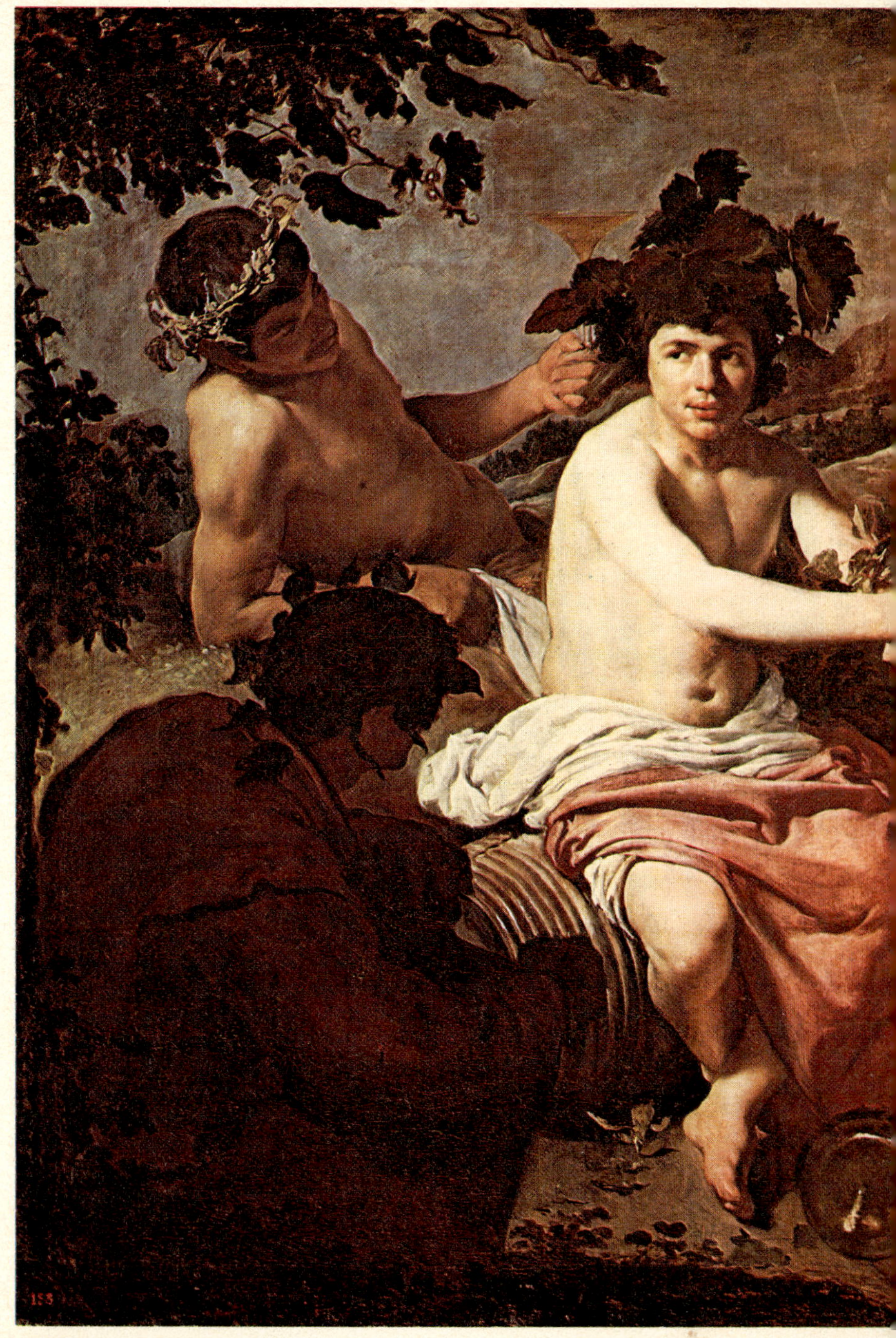

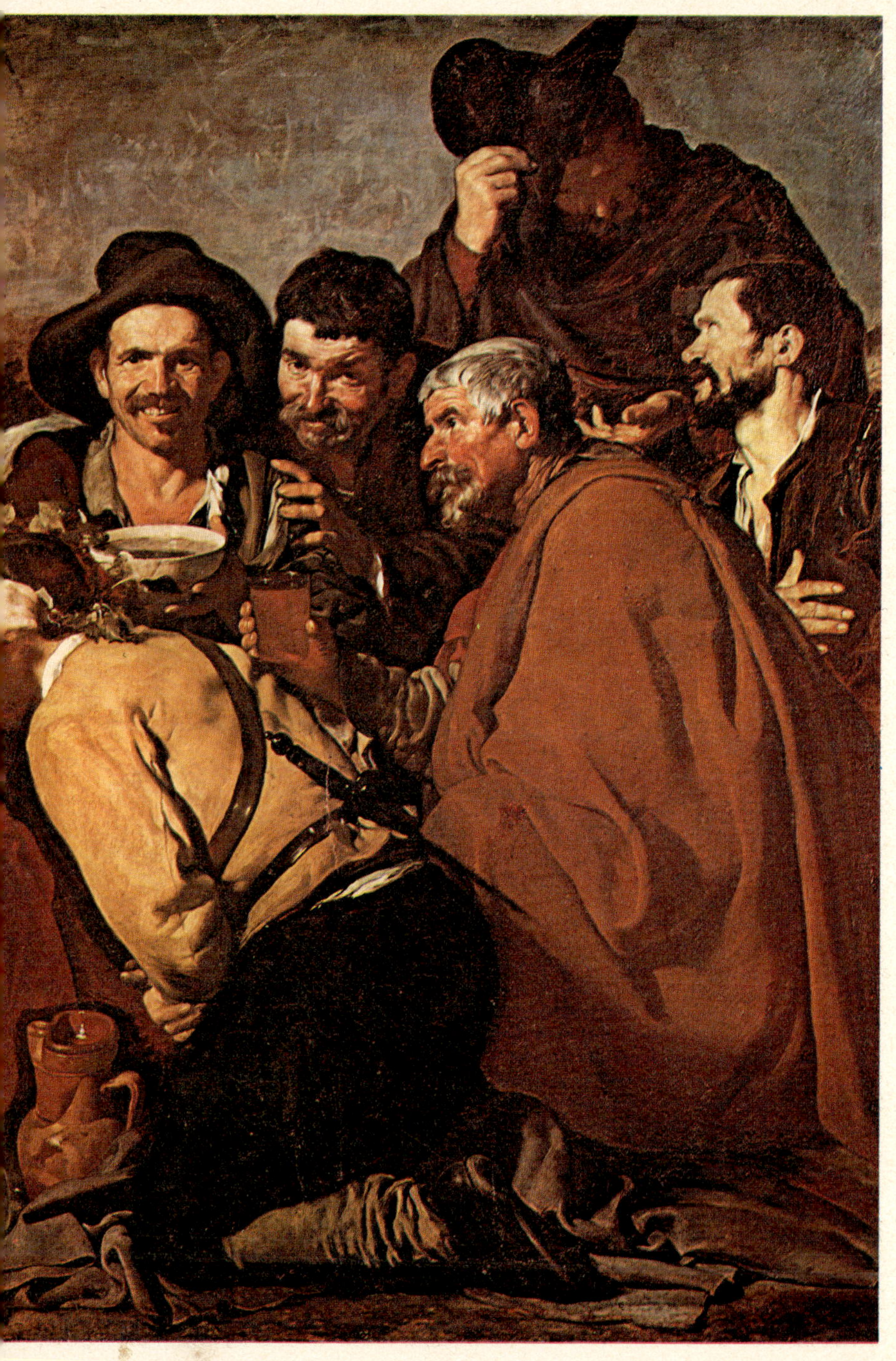

27 Philip IV *(bust)*
Oil on canvas/60.8 × 47.3/ 1623
Dallas, The Meadows Museum

28 Portrait of a Man*
Oil on canvas/52 × 40/ 1623 (?)
Detroit, Institute of Arts

29 Philip IV *(full-length)*
Oil on canvas/200 × 103/1624
New York, Metropolitan Museum of Art

30 Gaspar de Guzmán, Conde Duque de Olivares
Oil on canvas/202 × 107/1624
São Paulo, Museu de Arte

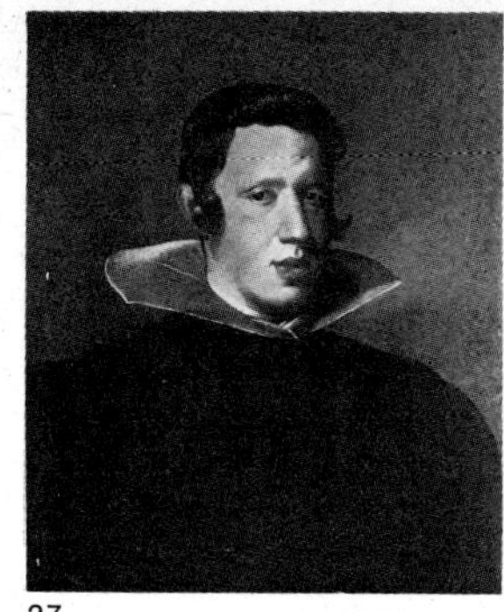
27

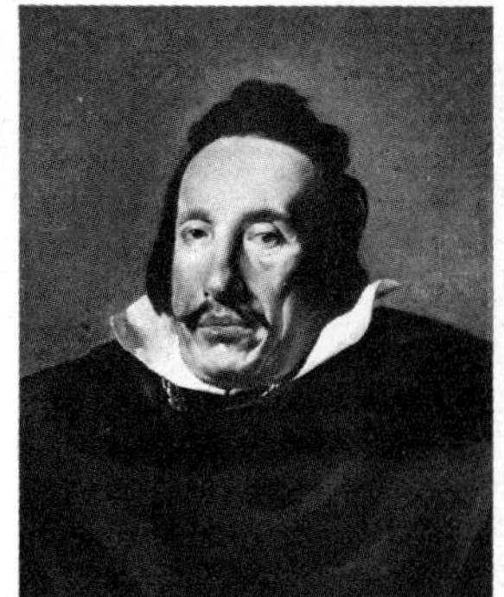
28

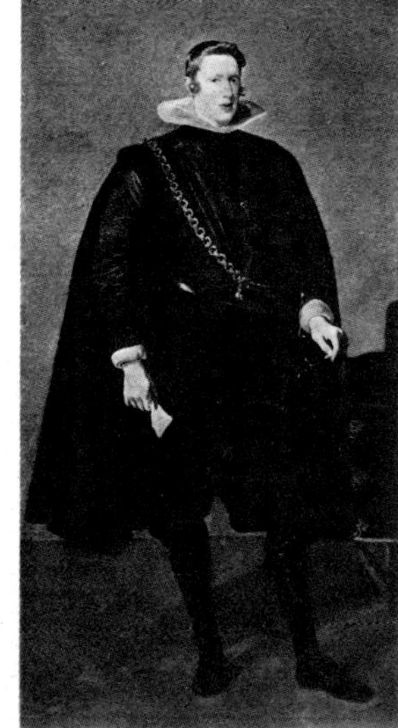
29

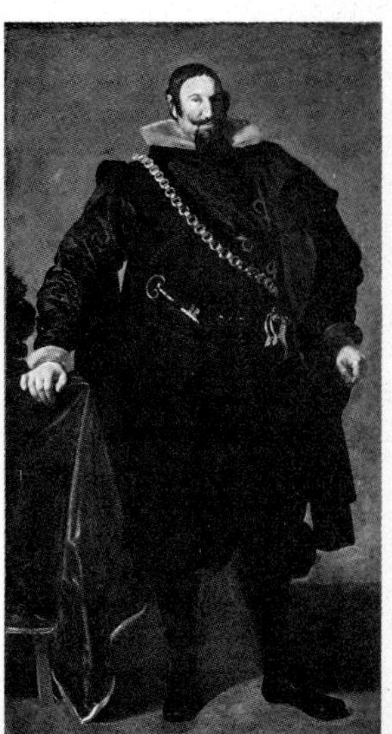
30

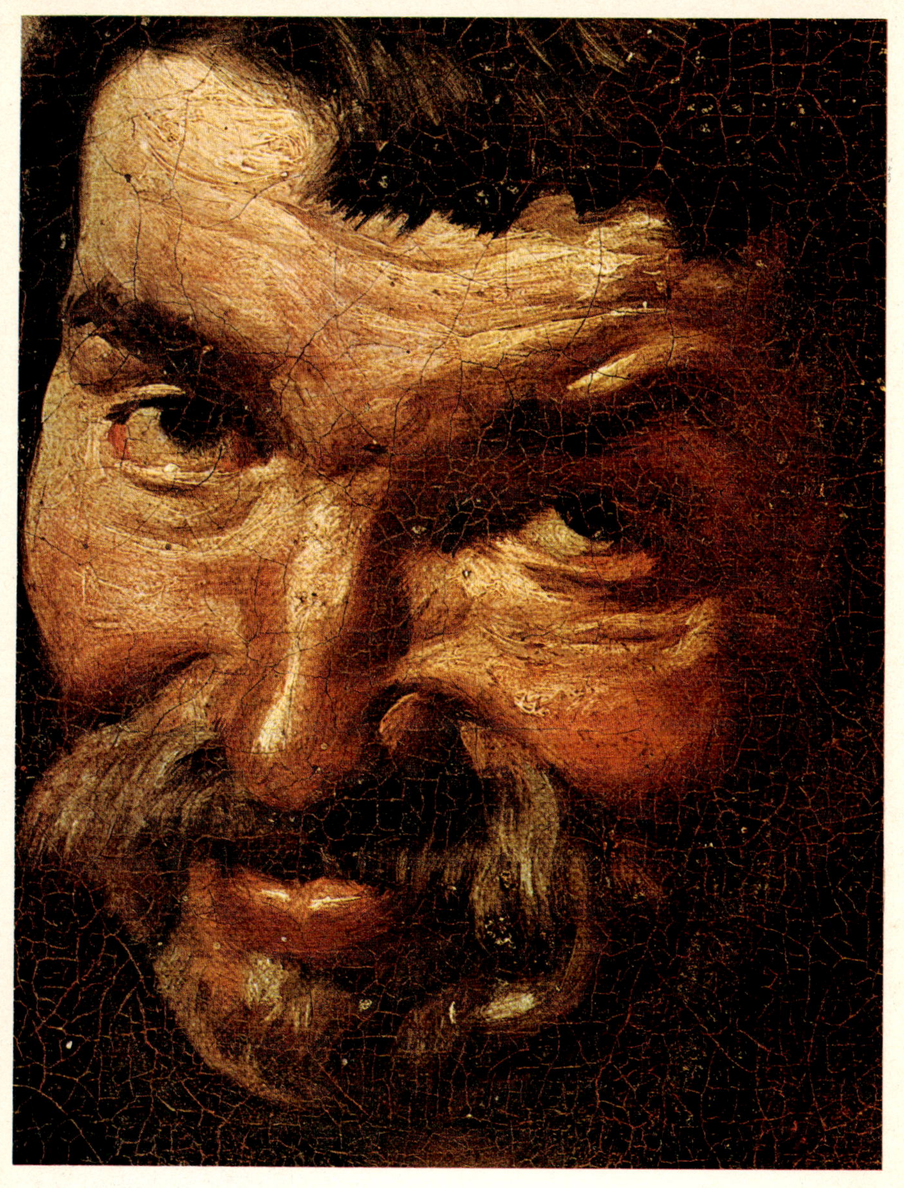

Bacchus (*No. 39, detail*).

31 Gaspar de Guzmán, Conde Duque de Olivares
Oil on canvas/216 × 129/1625
New York, Hispanic Society of America

32 A Lady
Oil on canvas/32 × 24/1625
Madrid, Palacio de Oriente

33 The Infante Don Carlos
Oil on canvas/209 × 125/ 1626–8
Madrid, Prado

34 Calabazas
Oil on canvas/175 × 106/ 1626–8
Cleveland (Ohio), Museum of Art

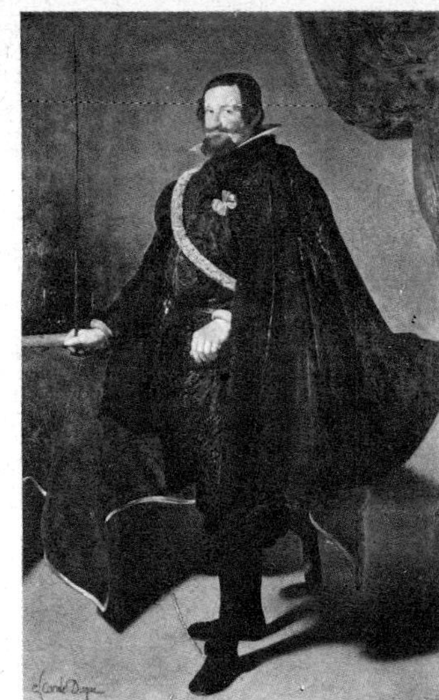

31

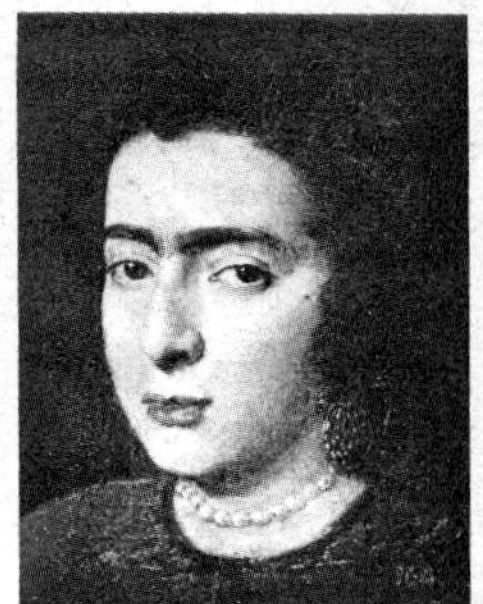

32

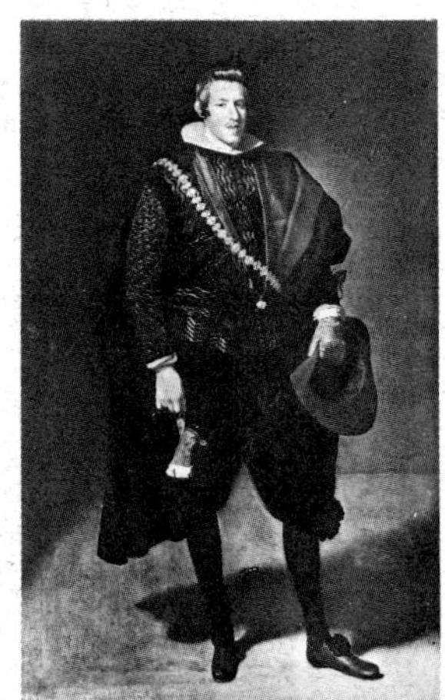

33

***The Forge of Vulcan* (*No. 43, detail*).**
The tone of the composition is set by the contrast between Apollo, a figure of idealized beauty, and the more down-to-earth vigorously modelled forms of Vulcan and his assistants. Compared with the Bacchus *these figures are more confidently placed in space, in attitudes which convey their astonishment at the god's sudden arrival. Velázquez has chosen solutions which clearly reflect his recent study of Italian Renaissance painters, especially in this case Raphael.*

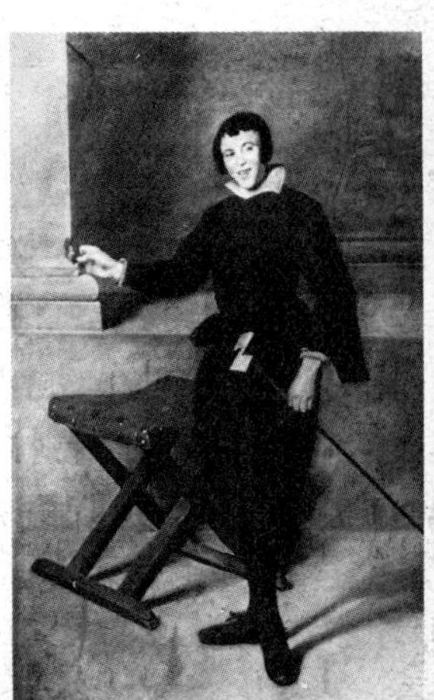

34

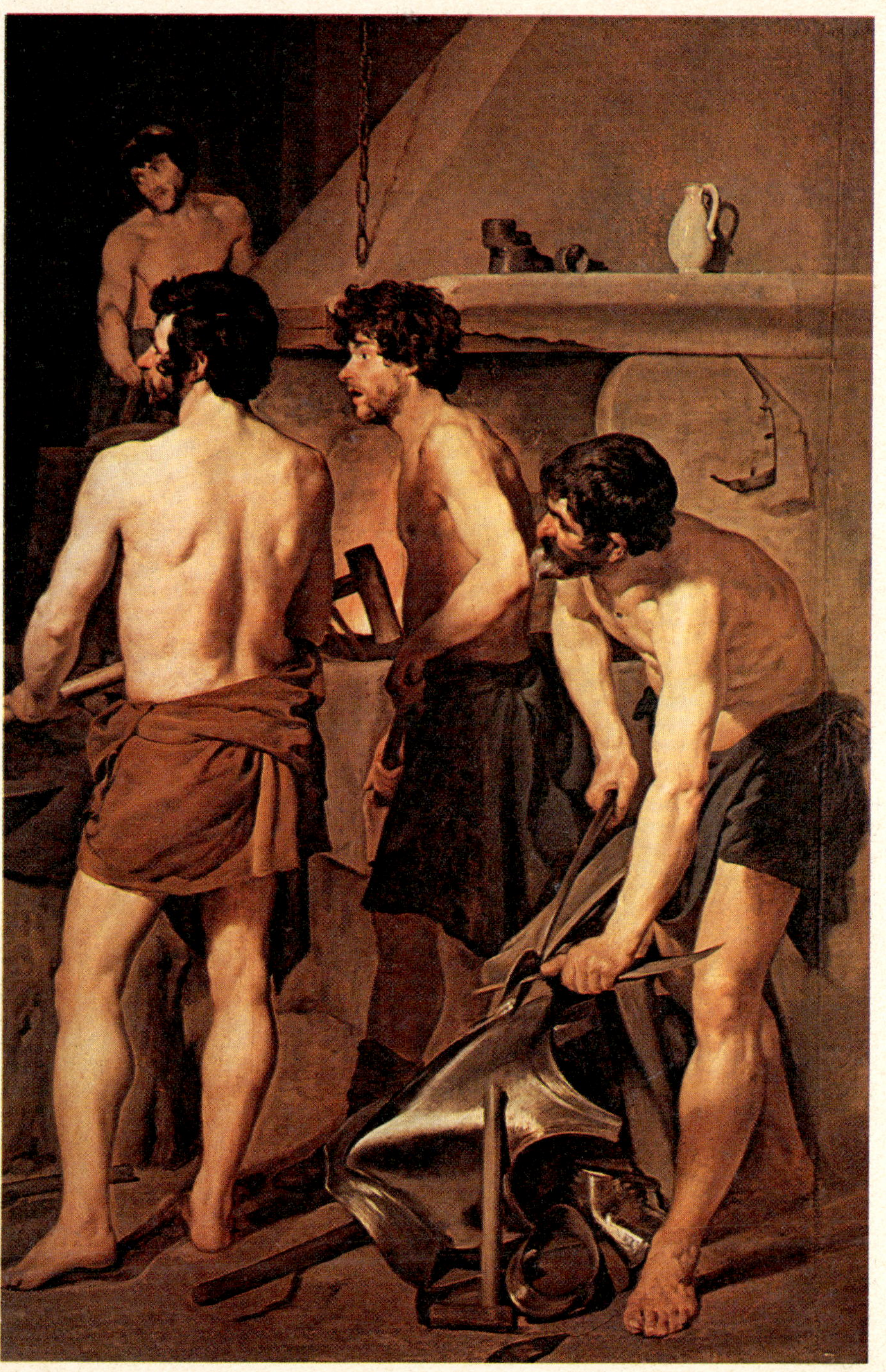

35 Philip IV *(bust, in armour)*
Oil on canvas/57 × 44/
1625–8
Madrid, Prado

36 Philip IV *(full-length)*
Oil on canvas/201 × 102/
1626–8
Madrid, Prado

37 Christ after the Flagellation contemplated by the Christian Soul
Oil on canvas/165 × 206/
1626–8
London, National Gallery

38 Portrait of a Young Man
(three-quarter length)
Oil on canvas/89.2 × 69.5/
1627–8
Munich, Alte Pinakothek

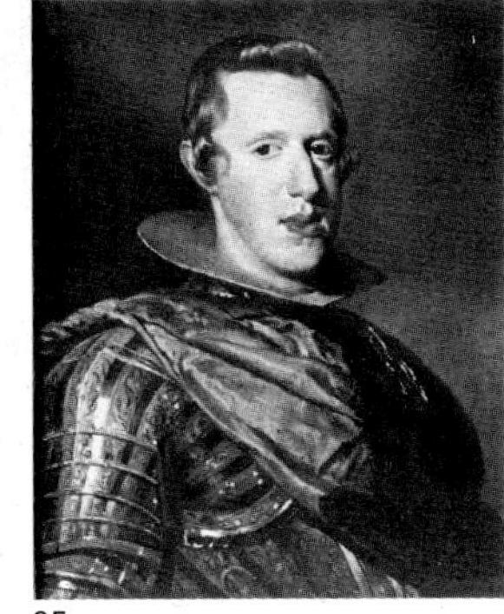
35

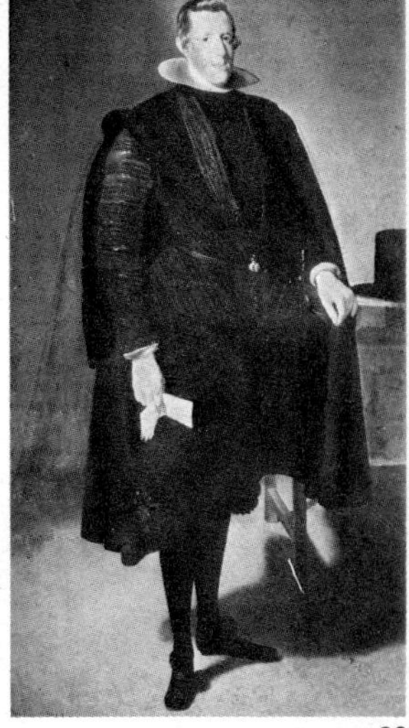
36

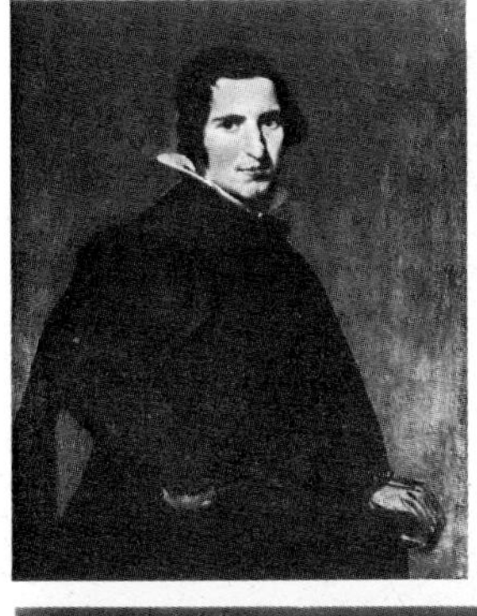
38

37
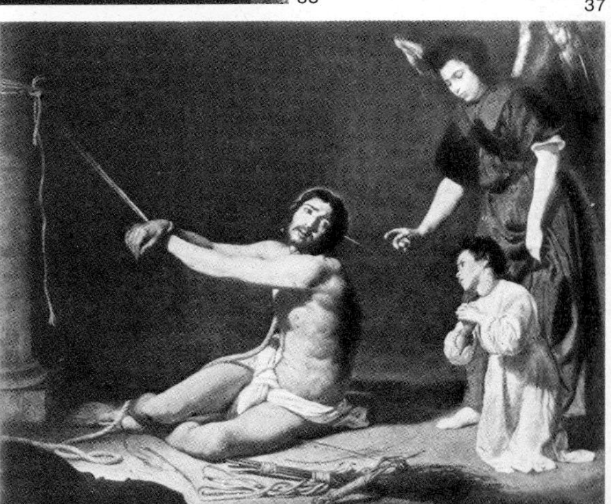

The Infanta Doña Maria, Queen of Hungary **(*No. 44*).**
A portrait of Philip IV's sister, born in 1606, who married Ferdinand III, King of Hungary, in 1631. According to Pacheco and Palomino Velázquez painted it in Naples, probably in Ribera's studio, in 1630 while the infanta was staying there on her way to Hungary.

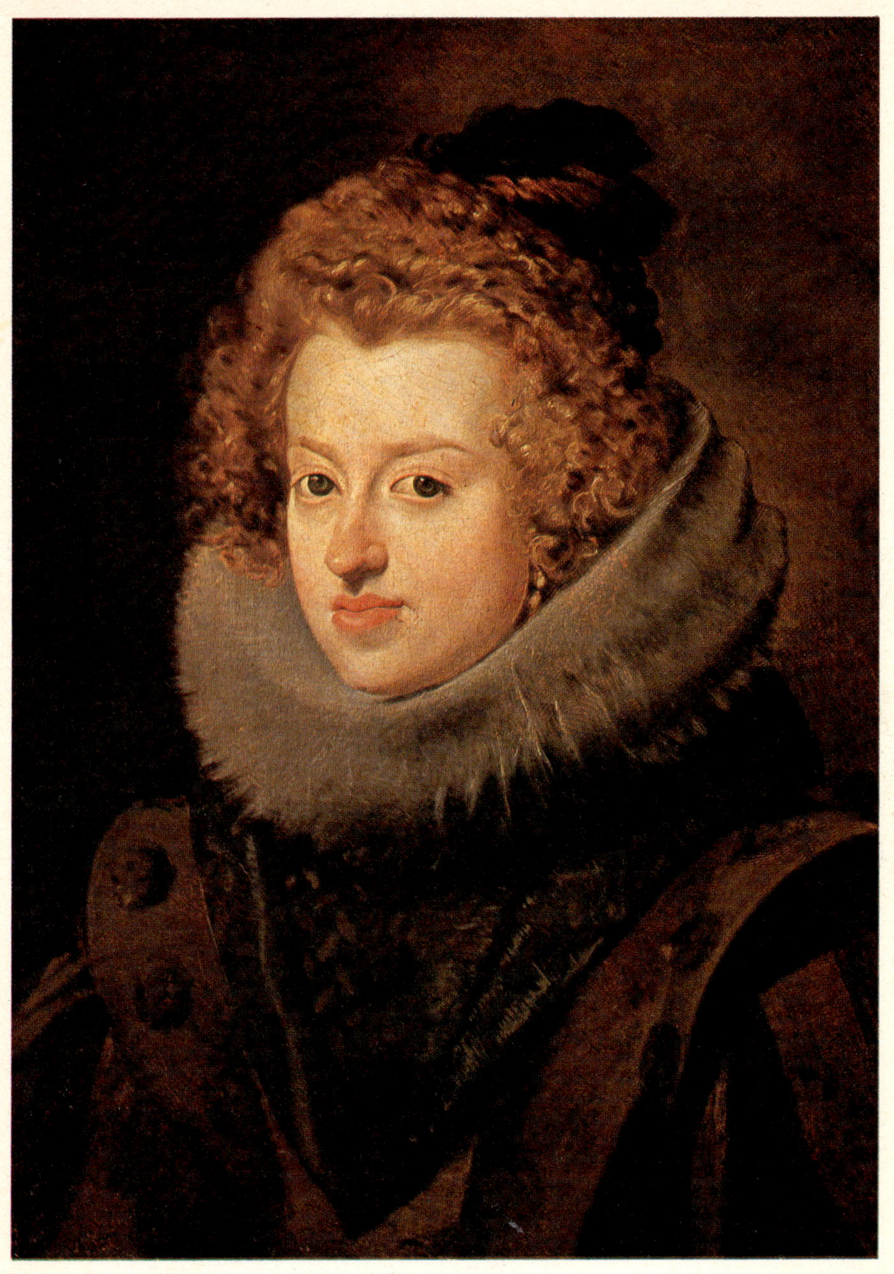

***39 Bacchus* ('*Los Borrachos*')**
Oil on canvas/165 × 225/1628
Madrid, Prado

***40 Democritus* (*the 'Geographer*')**
Oil on canvas/101 × 81/1628–40
Rouen, Musée des Beaux-Arts

41 Joseph's Bloody Coat brought to Jacob
Oil on canvas/223 × 250/1630
El Escorial, Monasterio

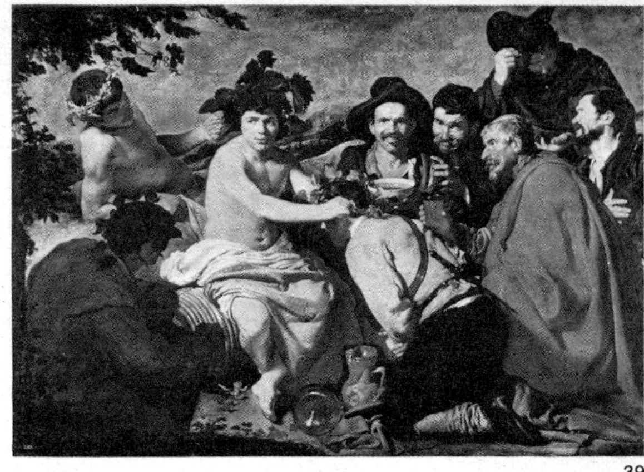

39

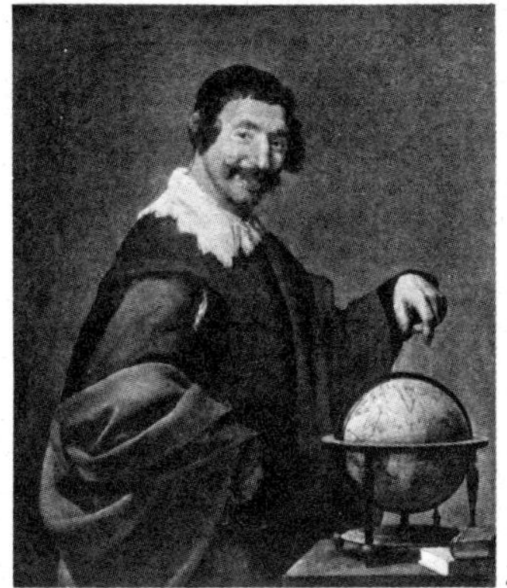

40

41

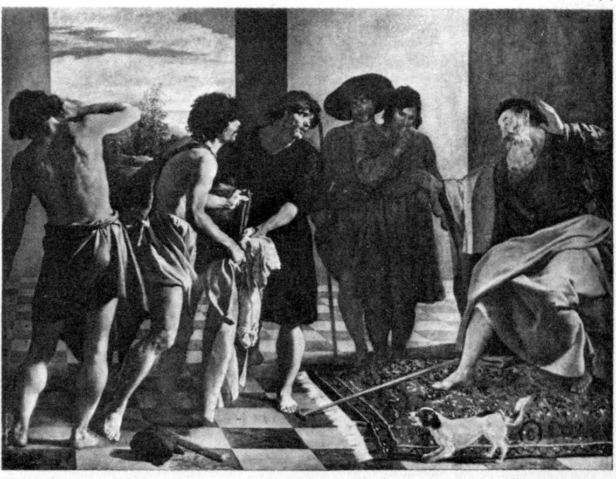

***Christ on the Cross* (*No. 46*).** *Believed by different scholars to date from either just before Velázquez' journey to Italy or soon after 1630. The formal qualities of the figure of Christ, his almost Apollonian beauty according to some writers, suggest it more probably belongs to the later date. The monumental quality of the work, and its solemn and carefully worked-out compositional scheme seem to bear this out.*

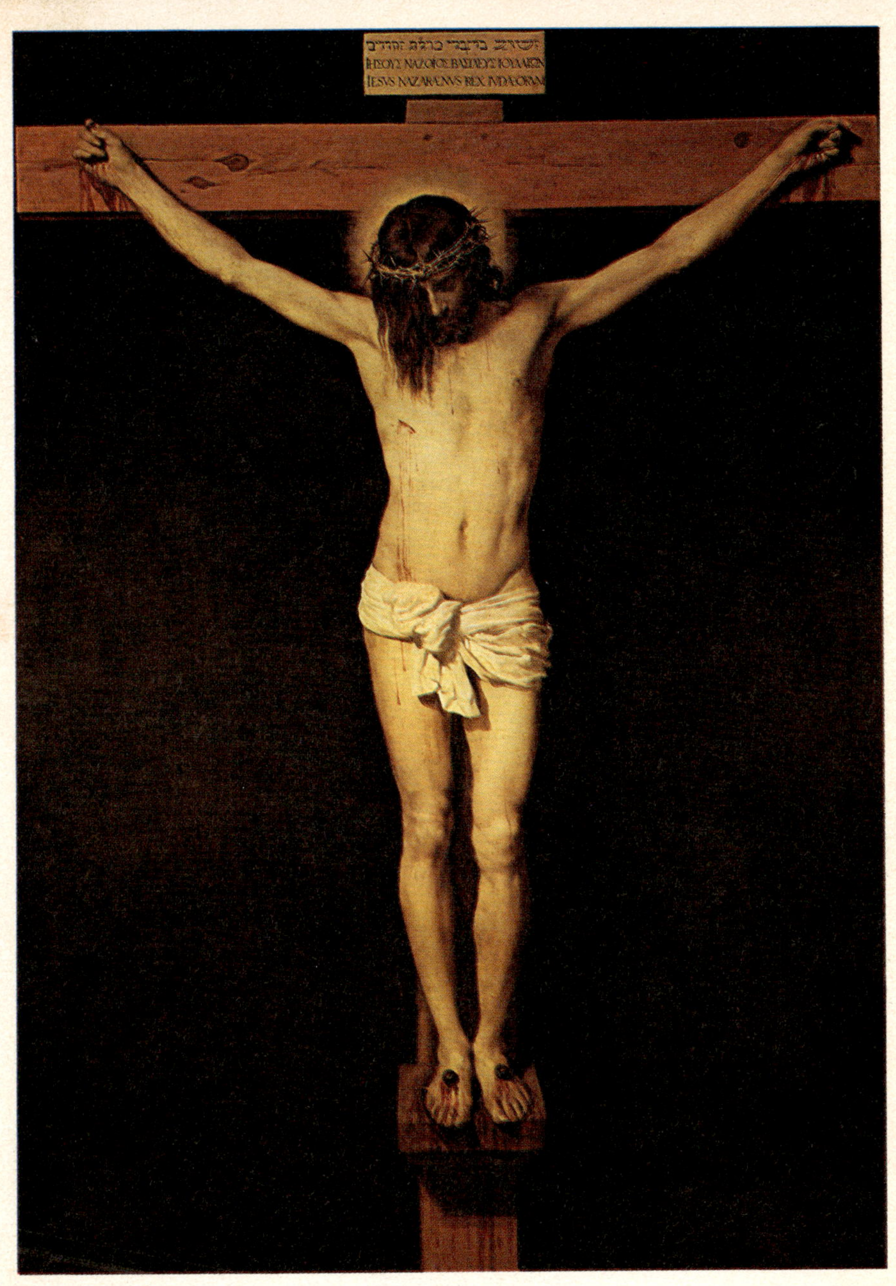
IESVS NAZARAENVS REX IVDAEORVM

42 Head of Apollo
Oil on canvas/36 × 25/1630
New York, Art Market
Probably a study for No. 43

43 The Forge of Vulcan
Oil on canvas/223 × 290/1630
Madrid, Prado

44 The Infanta Doña Maria, Queen of Hungary
Oil on canvas/58 × 44/1630
Madrid, Prado

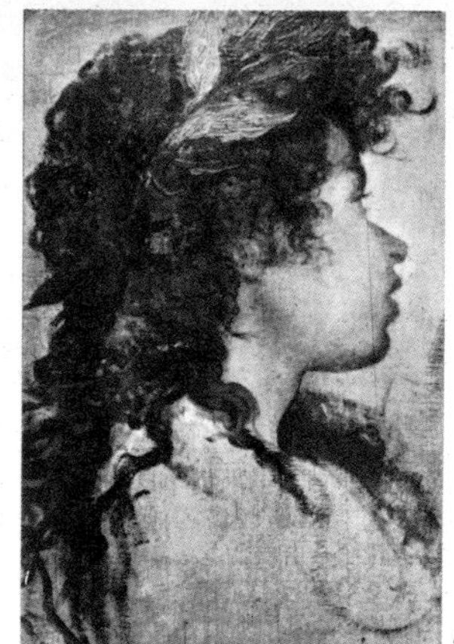

42

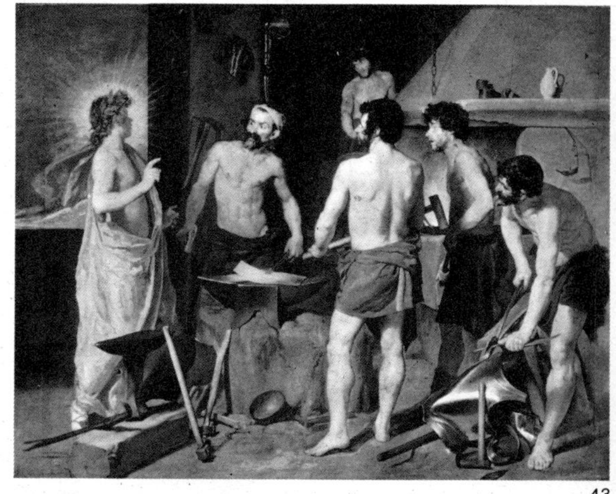

43

***Prince Baltasar Carlos with a Dwarf* (*No. 47, detail*).**
Completed, according to Pacheco, in March 1631, but begun immediately after the painter's return from Italy, as the inscription giving the prince's age as one year and four months seems to confirm. During the eighteenth century the portrait was believed to be by Correggio, but was first attributed to Velázquez by Waagen in 1854.

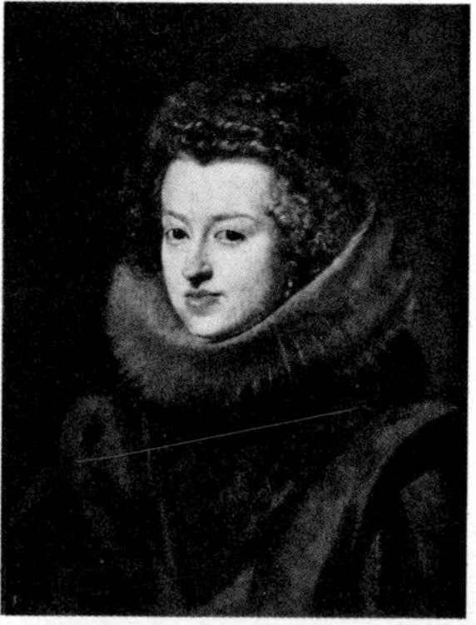

44

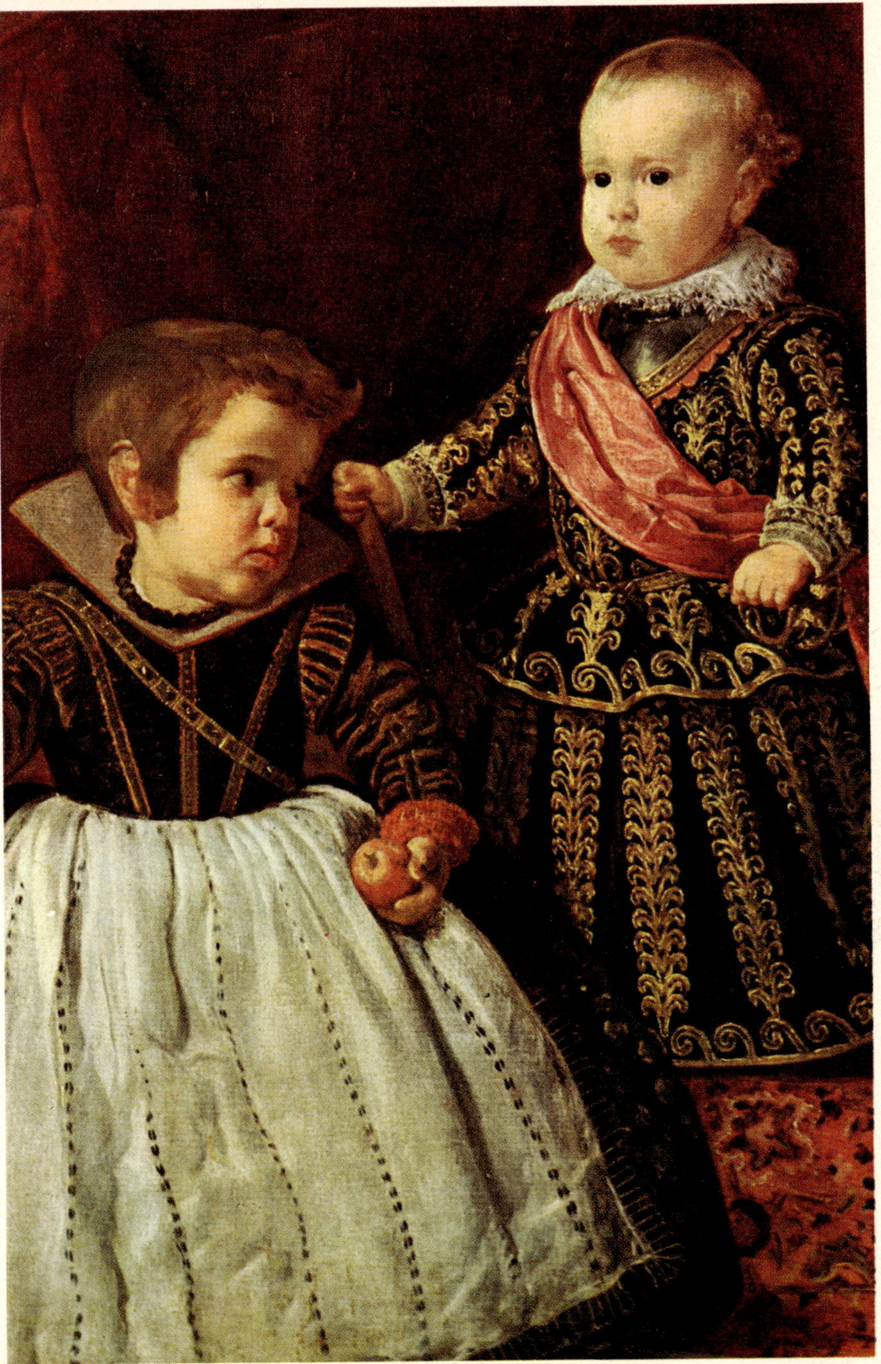

45 Gamblers in a Brawl
Oil on canvas/29 × 39.6/
1630 (?)
Rome, Galleria Pallavicini
This painting has been attributed to Velázquez, but the attribution is now refuted by specialists

***46 Christ on the Cross* (*'El Cristo de San Placido'*)**
Oil on canvas/248 × 169/
1630–32
Madrid, Prado

47 Prince Baltasar Carlos with a Dwarf
Oil on canvas/136 × 104/1631
Boston, Museum of Fine Arts

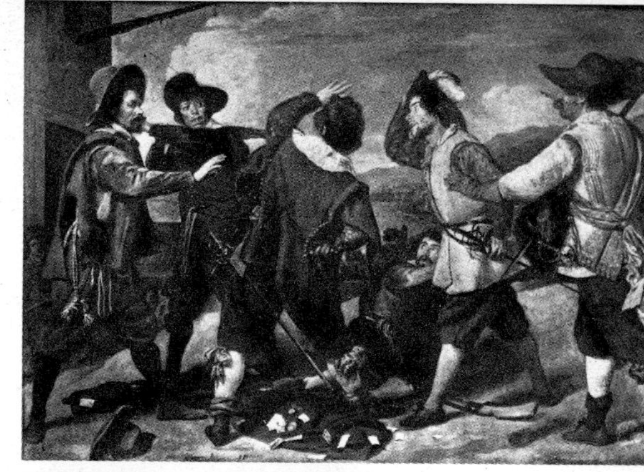

45

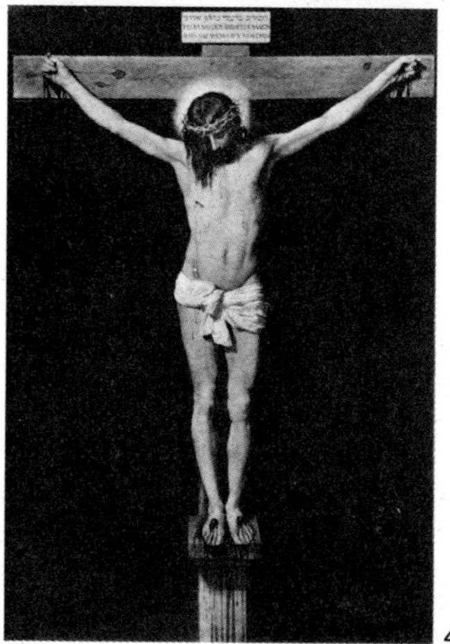

46

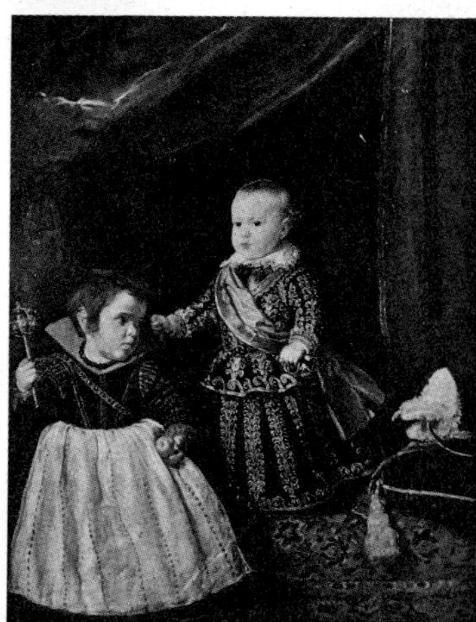

47

***Doña Antonia de Ipeñarrieta with One of her Sons* (*No. 48, detail*)**

A portrait of Pérez Araciel's widow, later the wife of Diego del Corral, painted in about 1631 and showing her with one of her children, probably Luís. She had previously commissioned other works by Velázquez and the portrait of her second husband, also in the Prado, is a companion piece to this one.

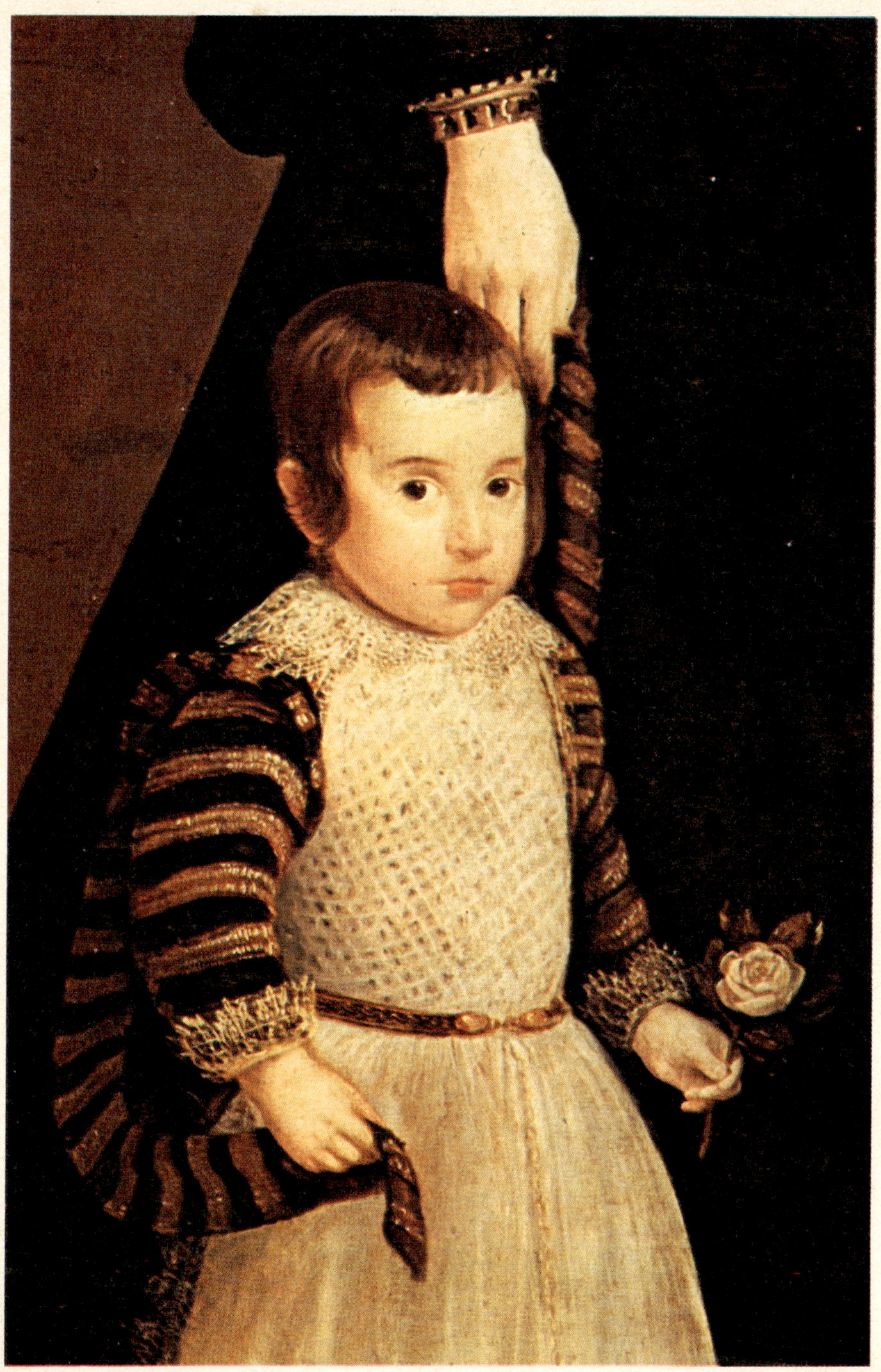

48 Doña Antonia de Ipeñarrieta with One of her Sons
Oil on canvas/215 × 110/1631
Madrid, Prado

49 Don Diego de Corral y Arellano
Oil on canvas/215 × 110/1631
Madrid, Prado

50 The Temptation of St Thomas Aquinas
Oil on canvas/244 × 203/1631 (?)
Orihuela (Alicante), Museo de la Santa Iglesia Catedral

48

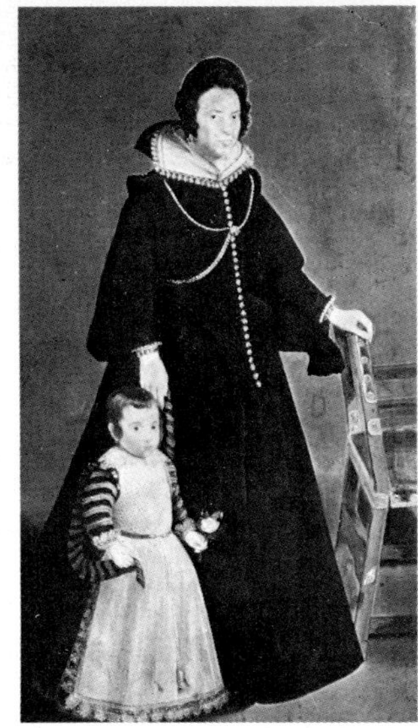

49

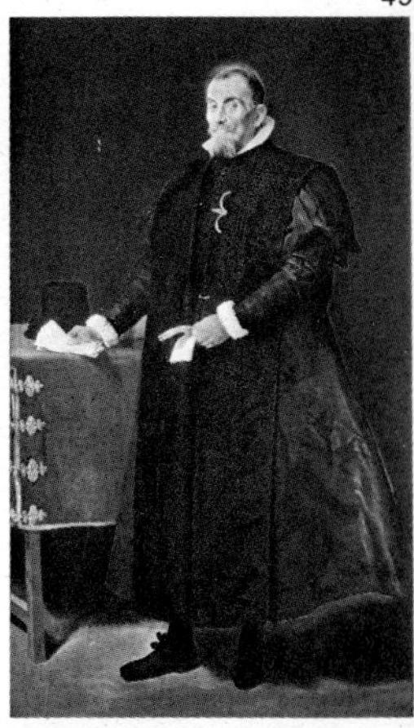

50

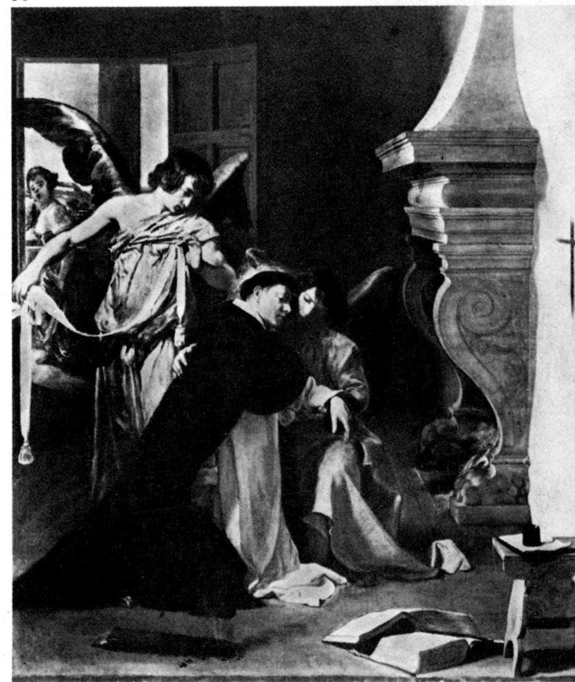

***Philip IV* (*No. 51*).**
This superb, full-length signed portrait is known as the 'Silver Philip' because of the striking silvery-grey tones of the king's clothes. It hung in the royal palace in Madrid until Joseph Bonaparte took it for one of his generals. Eventually the National Gallery, London, bought it in 1882.

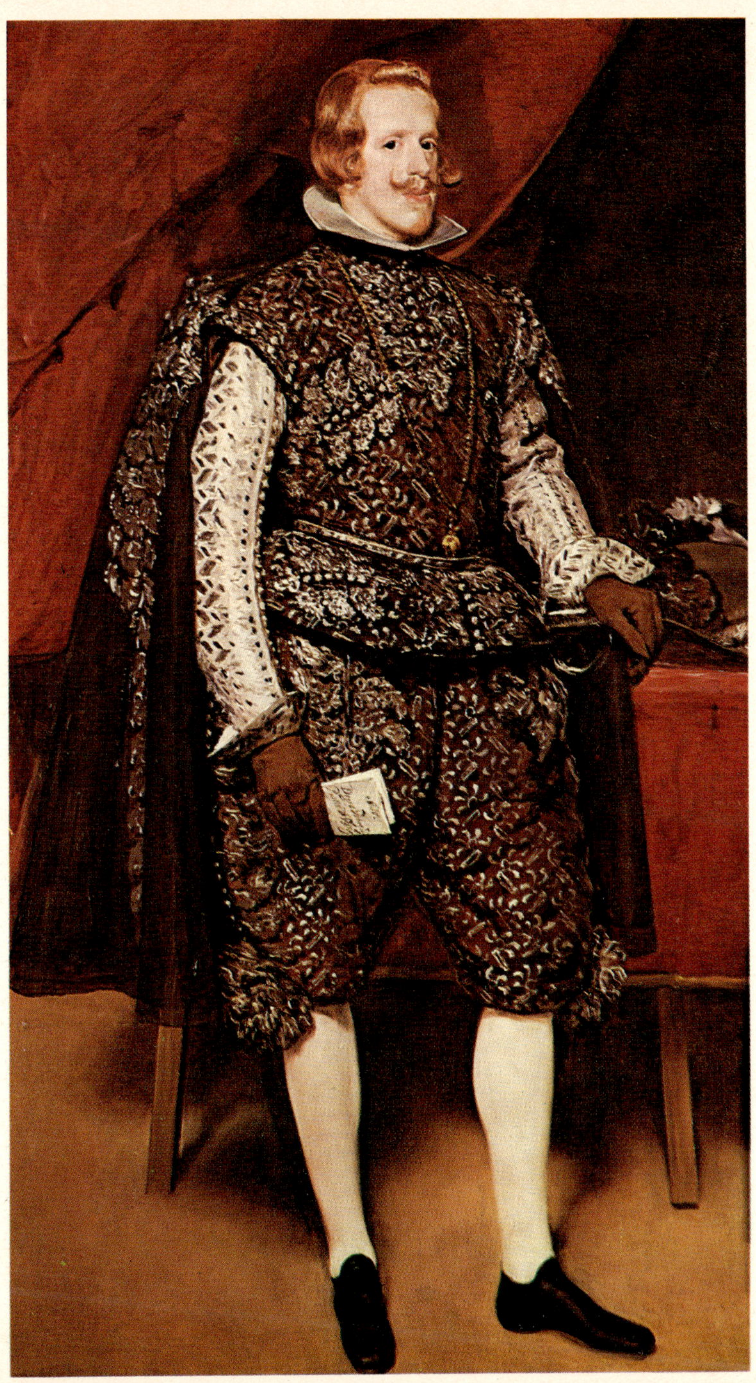

***The Surrender of Breda* (No. 65).**

The painting celebrates the capture of the Dutch stronghold of Breda on 2 June 1625, during the Thirty Years War, by Spanish troops under the Genoese general Ambrosio Spínola. The main problem facing Velázquez was how to bring together two large groups of figures and compose the perspective planes behind them to create a sense of spatial depth, transcending the limitations of a two-dimensional canvas, varying and enriching the compositional patterns of academic tradition. He found his solution in apparently simple compositional schemes carefully worked out down to the smallest detail, to create a luminous, airy whole, which foreshadows his mature achievements in The Maids of Honour *(No. 123) and* The Fable of Arachne *(No. 126).*

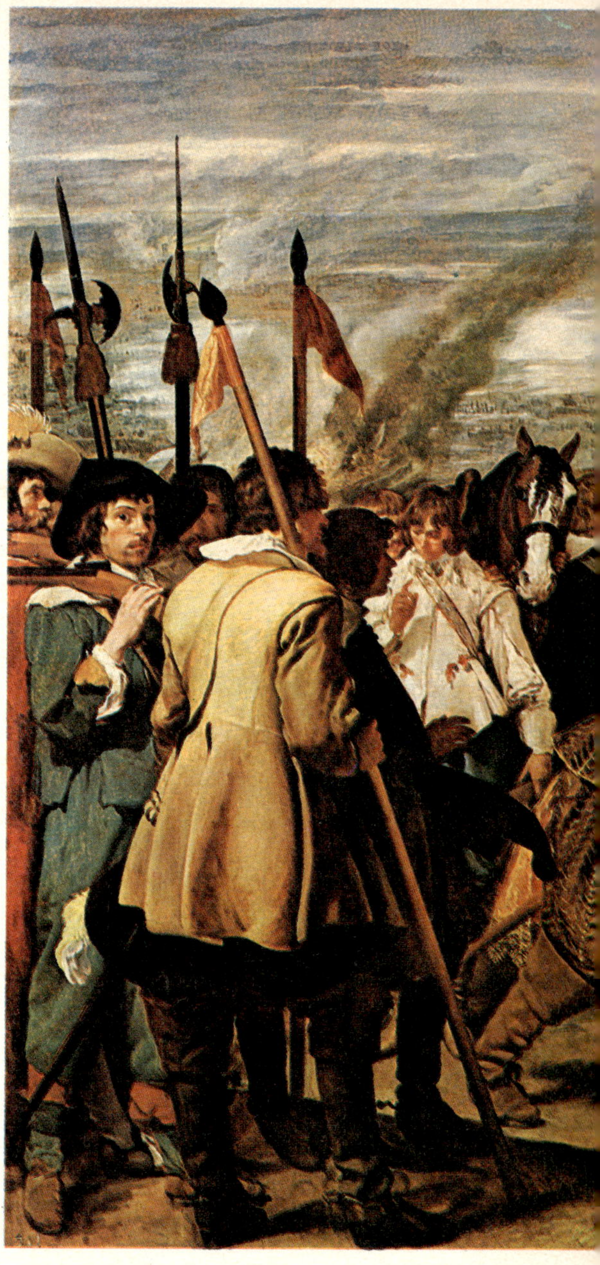

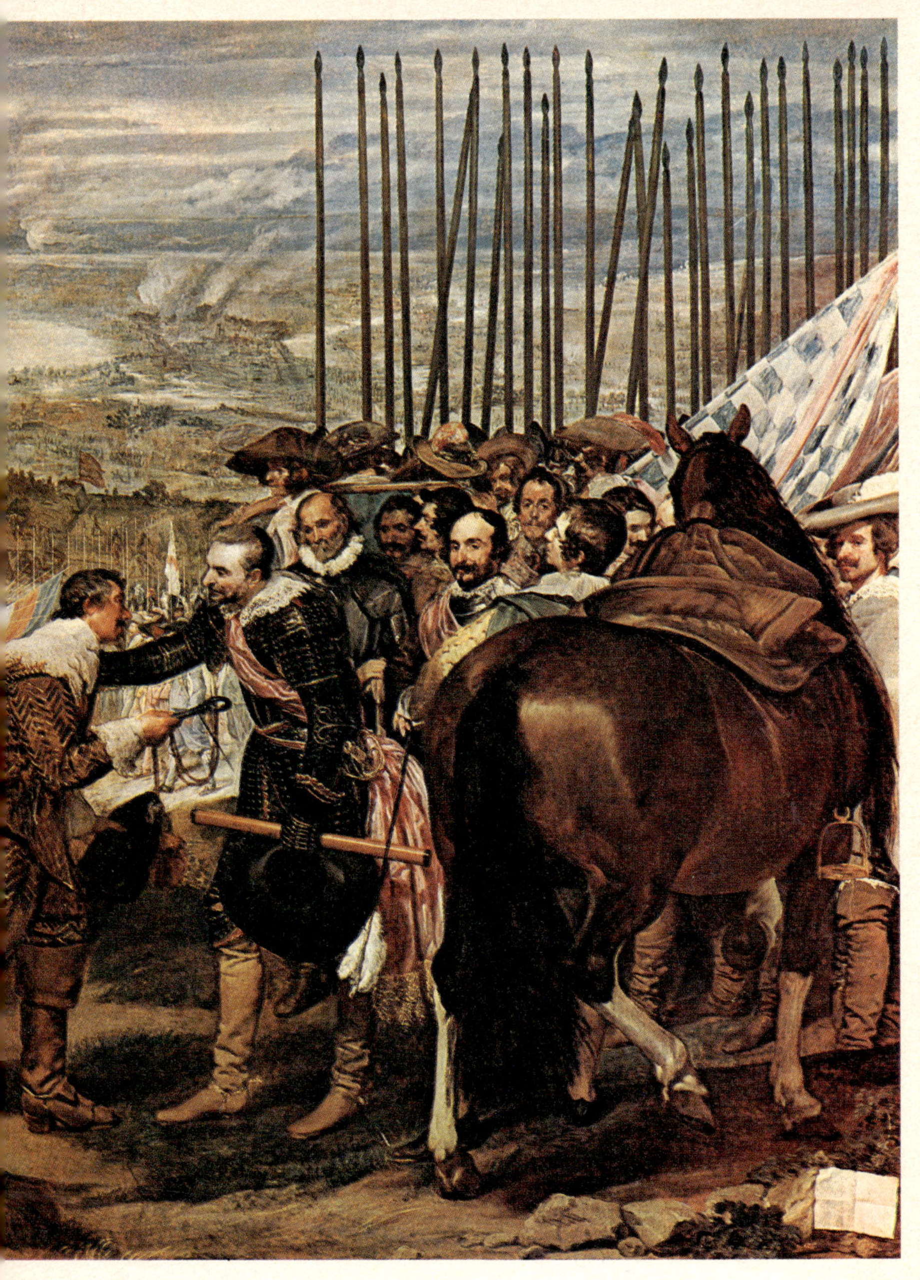

***51 Philip IV** (full-length)*
Oil on canvas/199.5 × 113/
s. 1631–2
London, National Gallery

52 Queen Isabel of Bourbon
Oil on canvas/203 × 114/
1631–2
Germany, Private Collection

53 A Knight of Calatrava
Oil on canvas/198.2 × 111.8/
1631–3
Europe, Private Collection

54 Philip IV
Oil on canvas/127.5 × 86/1632
Vienna, Kunsthistorisches
Museum

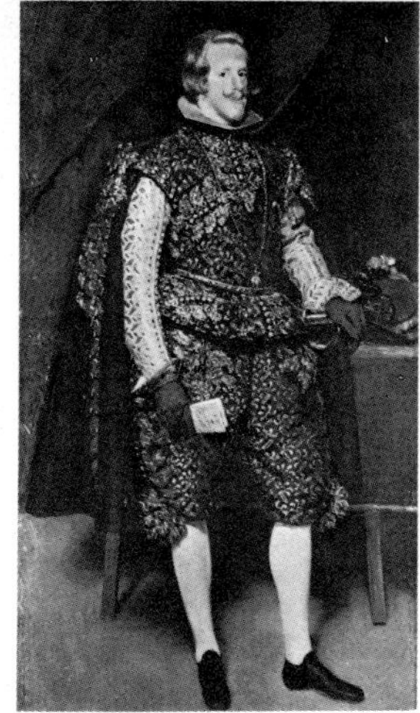
51

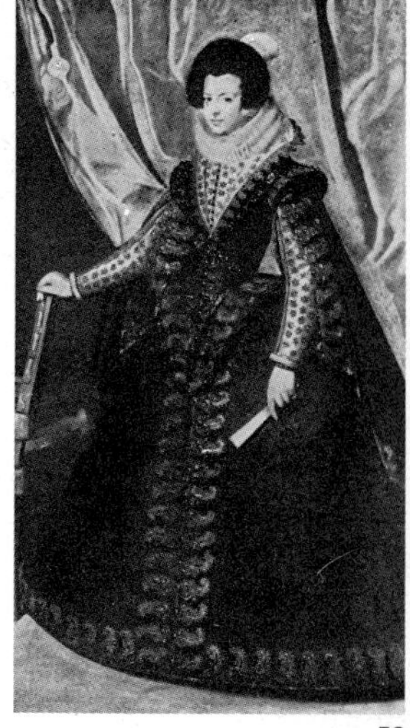
52

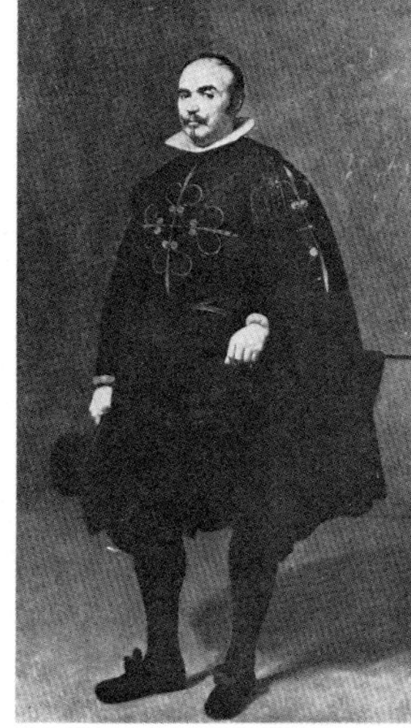
53

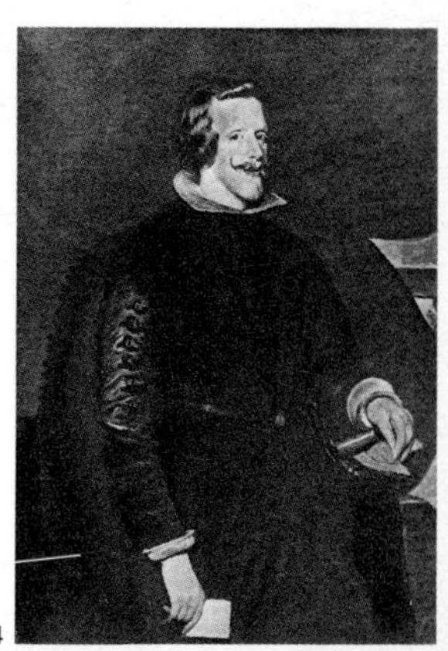
54

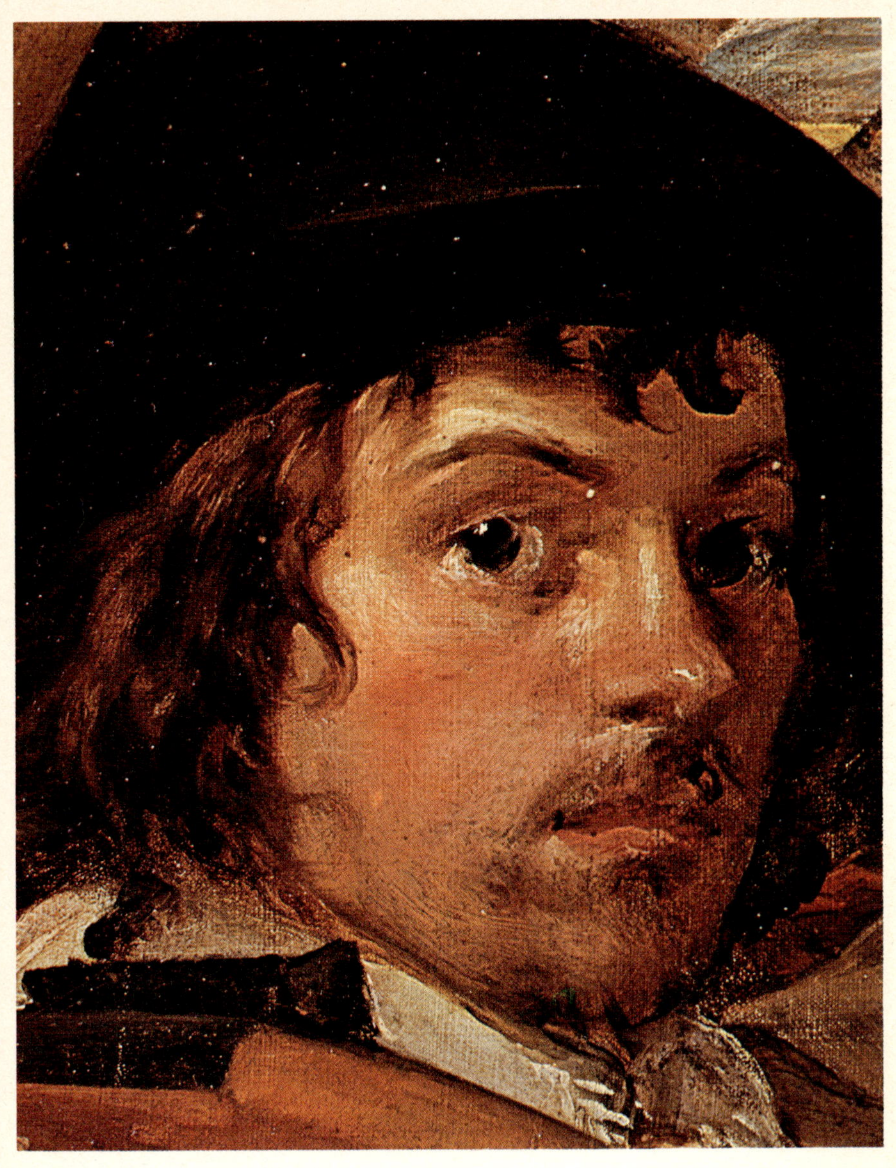

The Surrender of Breda
(No. 65, detail)

55 Queen Isabel
Oil on canvas/128.5 × 99.5/1632
Vienna, Kunsthistorisches Museum

56 Prince Baltasar Carlos (aged three)
Oil on canvas/118 × 95.5/1632
London, Wallace Collection

57 A Woman as a Sibyl (Juana Pacheco (?))
Oil on canvas/62 × 50/1632
Madrid, Prado

58 Don Juan Mateos
Oil on canvas/108.5 × 90/1632
Dresden, Gemäldegalerie

59 Philip IV as a Hunter
Oil on canvas/191 × 126/1632–3
Madrid, Prado

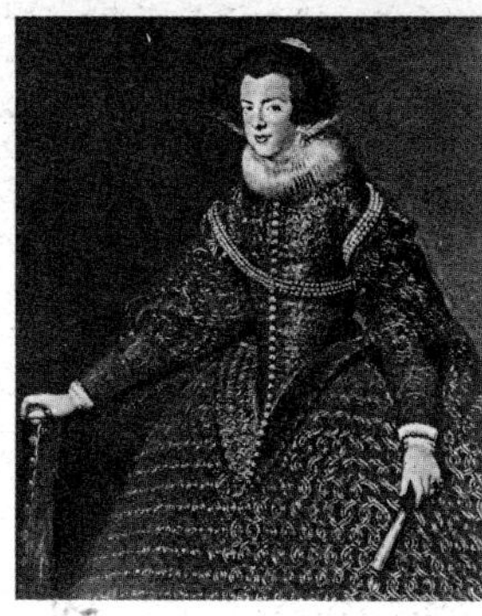
55

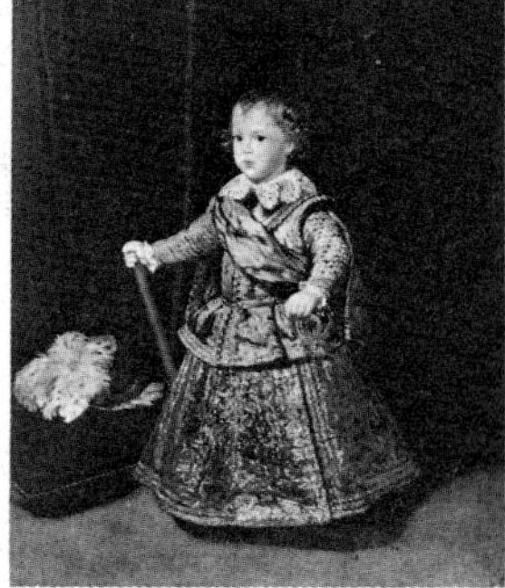

56

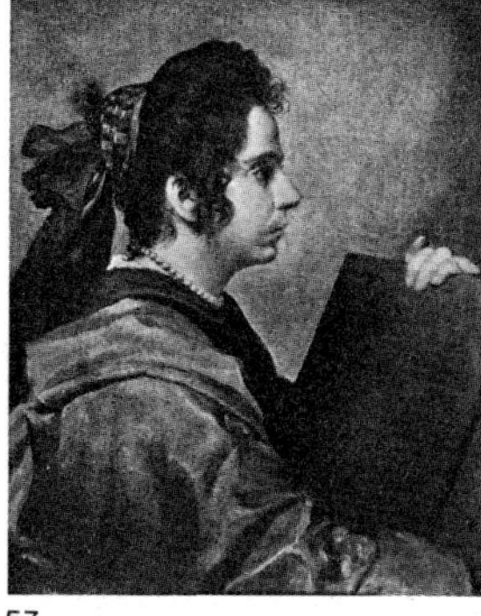
57

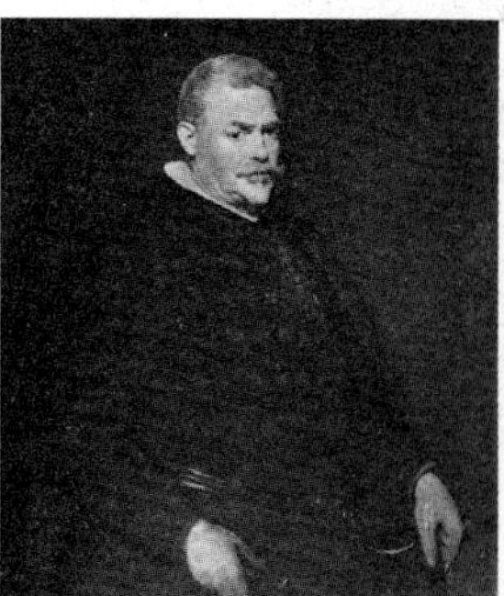
58

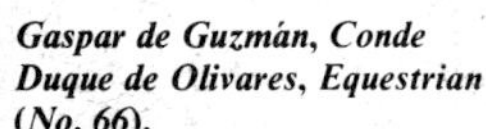
Gaspar de Guzmán, Conde Duque de Olivares, Equestrian (No. 66).
This work shows Philip IV's powerful chief minister and commander of the Spanish cavalry. It is one of many examples of Velázquez' ability to combine official portraiture with penetrating insight – pictorial rather than psychological – and present reality.

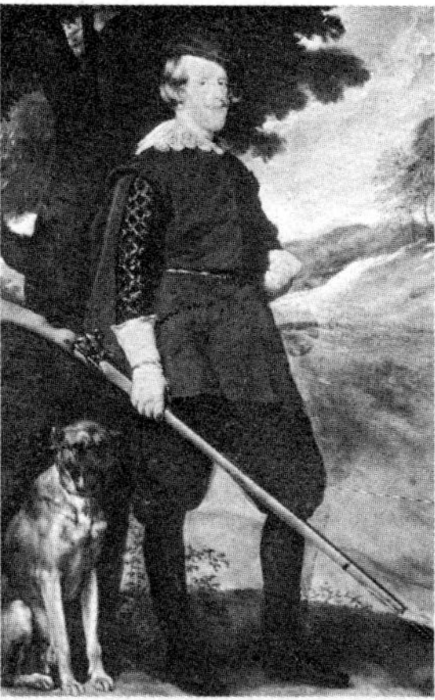
59

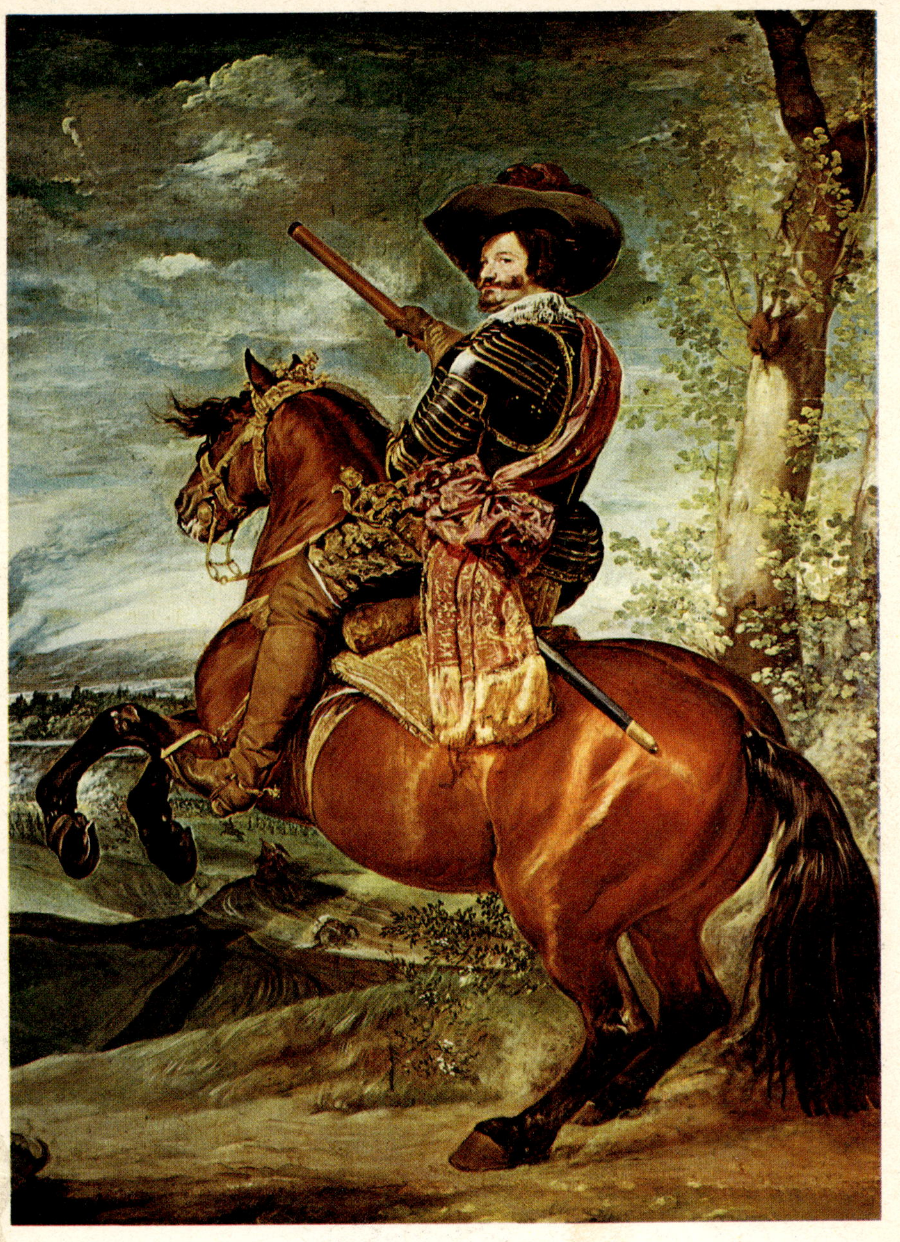

60 The Cardinal Infante Don Fernando as a Hunter
Oil on canvas/191 × 107/
1632–3
Madrid, Prado

61 Pablo de Valladolid*
Oil on canvas/209 × 123/
1632–4
Madrid, Prado

62 Philip III, Equestrian
Oil on canvas/300 × 314/
1629–35
Madrid, Prado

63 Queen Margarita of Austria, Equestrian
Oil on canvas/297 × 309/
1629–35
Madrid, Prado

64 Queen Isabel, Equestrian
Oil on canvas/301 × 314/
1629–35
Madrid, Prado

65 The Surrender of Breda
Oil on canvas/307 × 367/
1634–5
Madrid, Prado

66 Gaspar de Guzmán, Conde Duque de Olivares, Equestrian
Oil on canvas/313 × 239/
1634–5
Madrid, Prado

67 A White Horse
Oil on canvas/310 × 245/
1634–5
Madrid, Palacio Real

68 Philip IV, Equestrian
Oil on canvas/301 × 314/
1634–5
Madrid, Prado

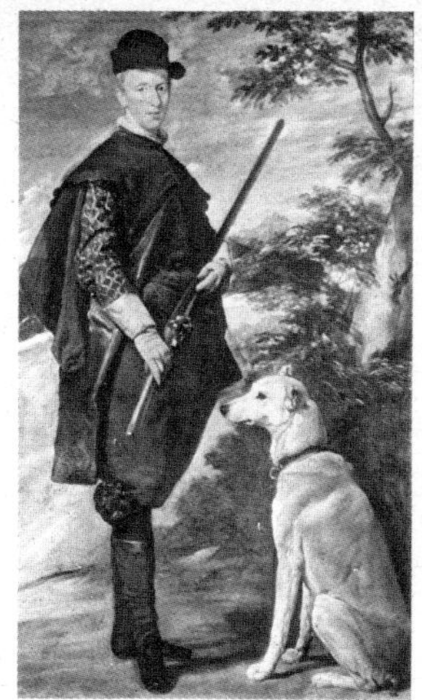

60

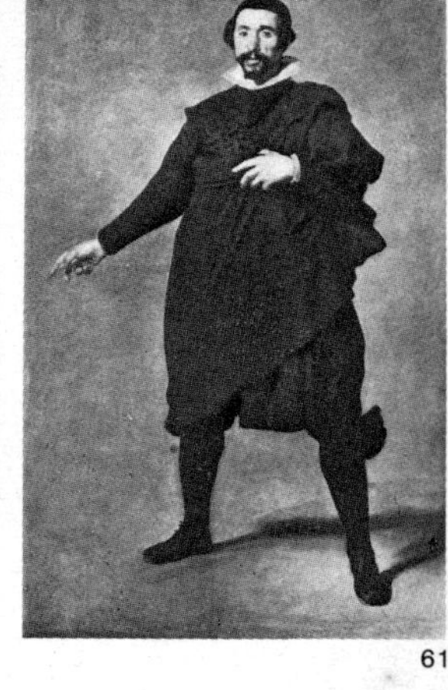

61

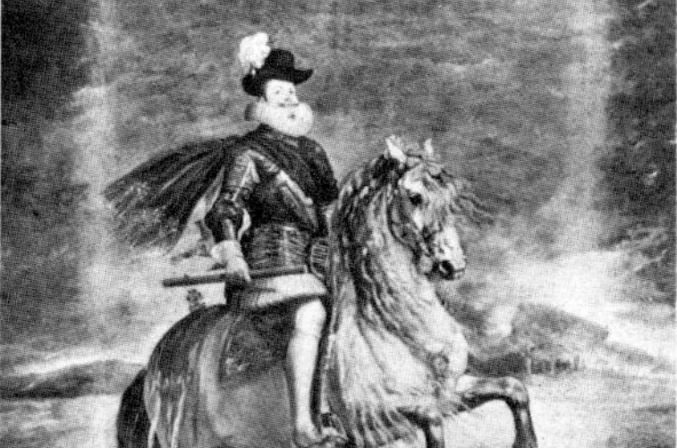

62

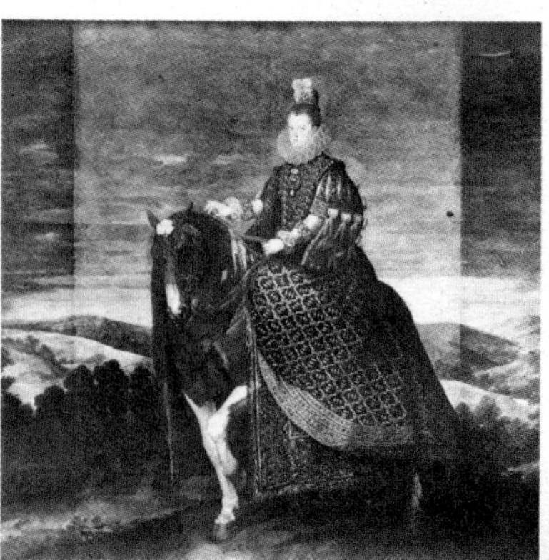

63

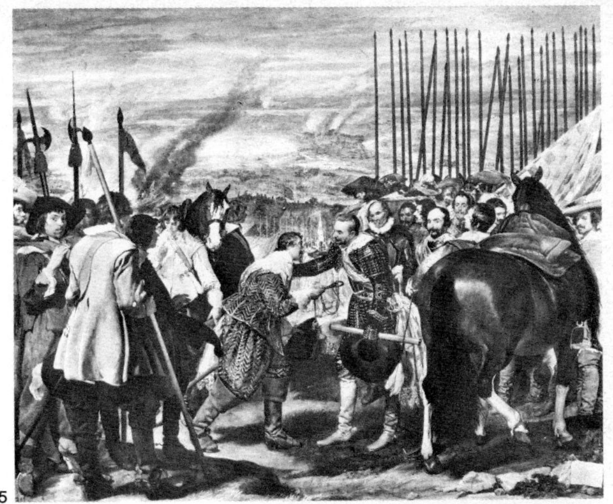
65

64
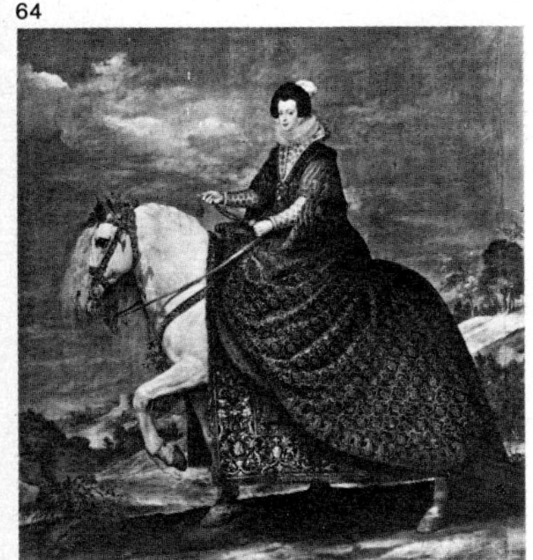

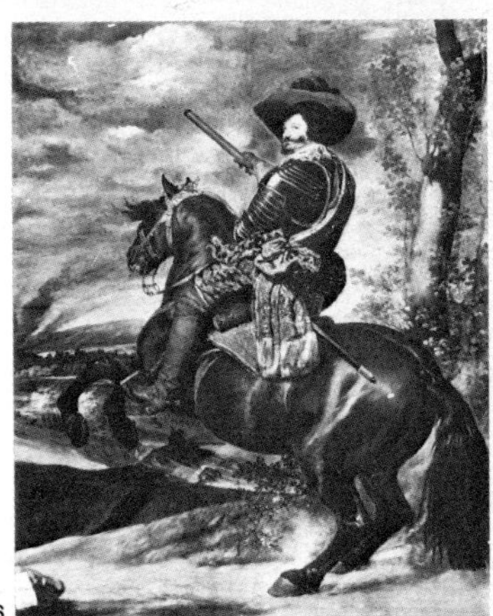
66

67
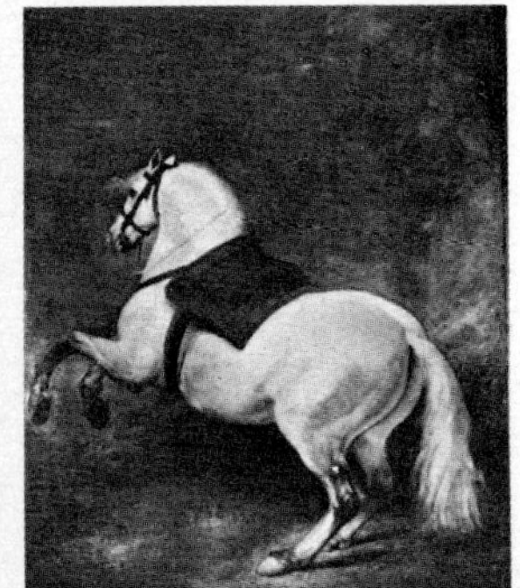

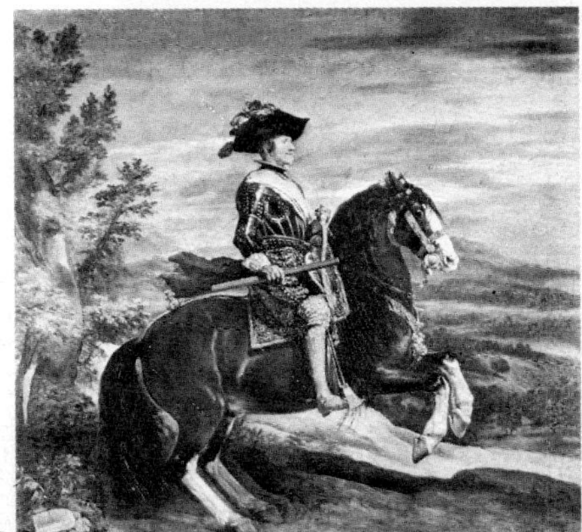
68

69 Prince Baltasar Carlos, Equestrian
Oil on canvas/209 × 173/1635
Madrid, Prado

70 Head of a Stag
Oil on canvas/66 × 52/1634–6
Madrid, De Baiguer Collection

71 Prince Baltasar Carlos as a Hunter
Oil on canvas/191 × 103/1635
Madrid, Prado

72 Don Cristóbal de Castañeda y Pernia ('Barbarroja')
Oil on canvas/198 × 121/1635 (?)
Madrid, Prado

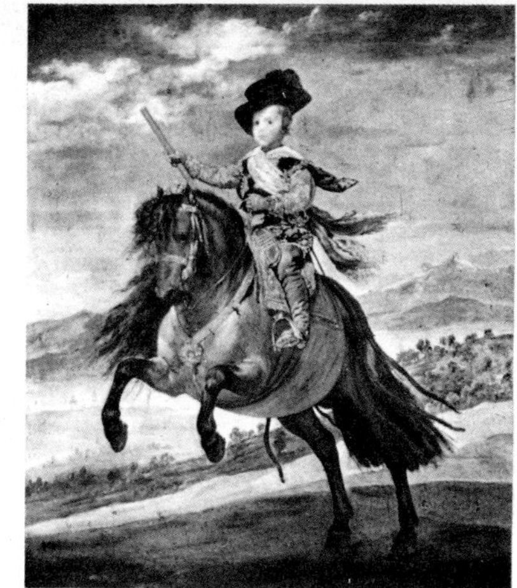
69

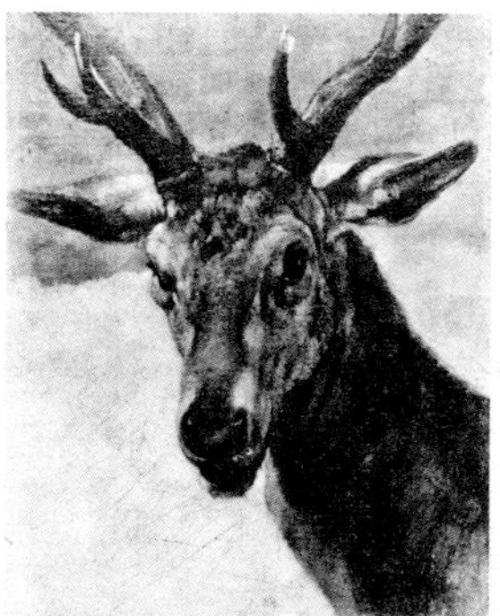
70

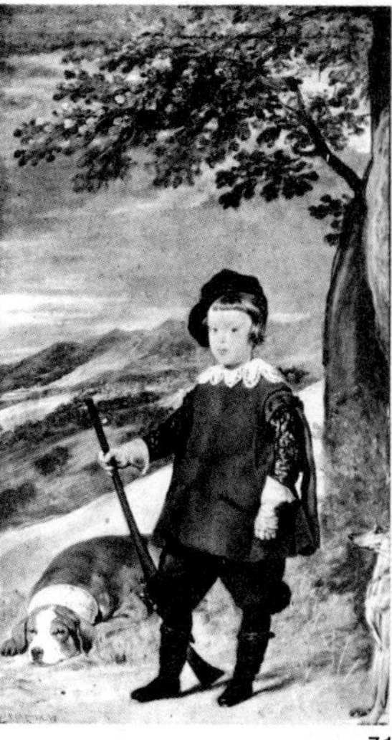
71

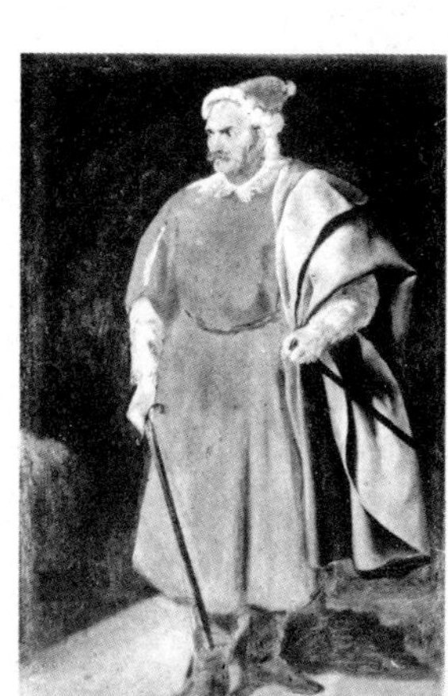
72

***Prince Baltasar Carlos, Equestrian* (*No. 69*).**
The outstanding qualities of this painting are epitomized in the placing of the child on his sturdy pony and the light and colour relationship between him and his natural setting. This setting is captured by the rendering of atmospheric values and the use of swift brush strokes of dense colour to suggest rather than reproduce exactly different aspects of the landscape.

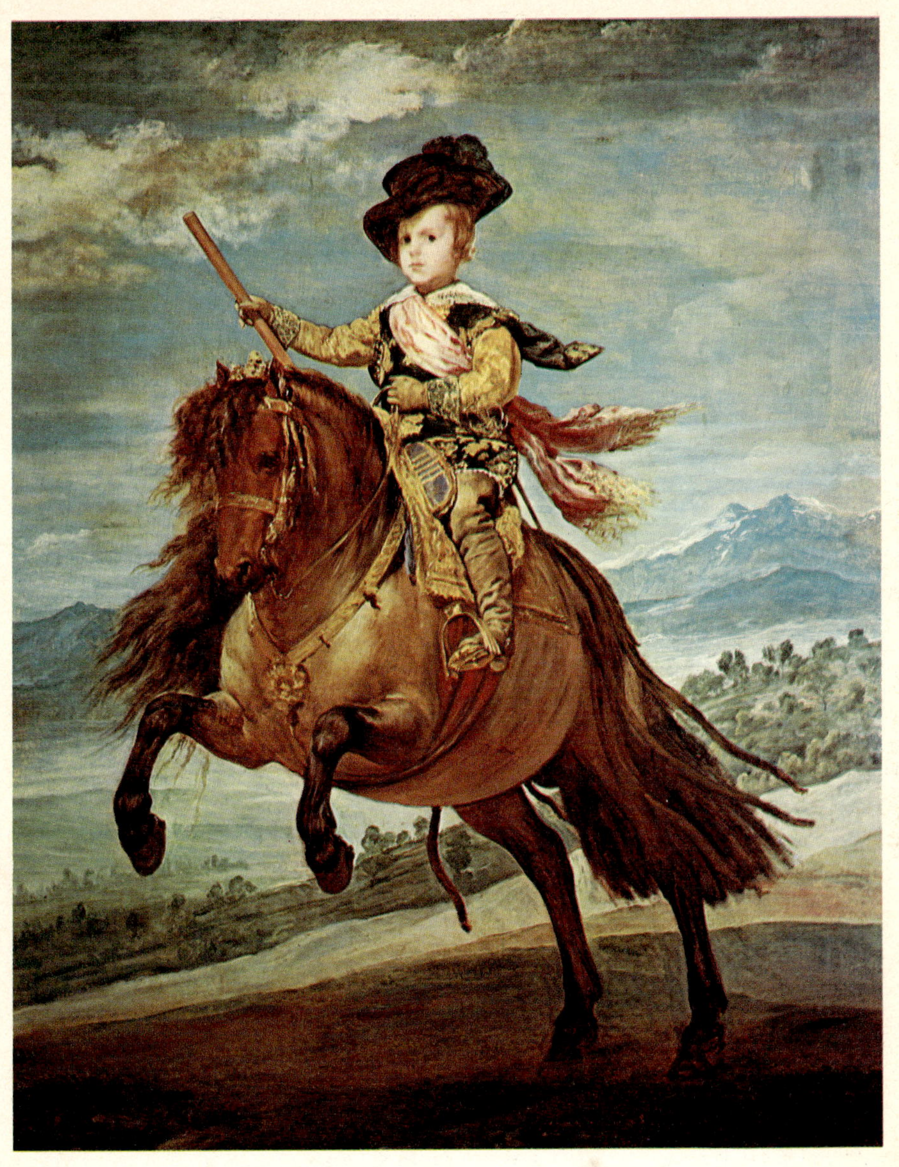

73 Prince Baltasar Carlos with the Conde Duque de Olivares at the Royal Mews*
Oil on canvas/145 × 96.5/1636
England, Grosvenor Estate

74 The Sculptor Martínez Montañes at Work
Oil on canvas/109 × 87/1636
Madrid, Prado

75 Gaspar de Guzmán, Conde Duque de Olivares
Oil on canvas/182 × 302/1638 (?)
Leningrad, Hermitage

76 The Royal Boar-hunt
Oil on canvas/182 × 302/1638 (?)
London, National Gallery
With an assistant

***Portrait of a Bearded Man* (*No. 77, detail*).**
The sitter has been variously identified as Velázquez himself, Calderón de la Barca, Antonio Pérez, Philip II's secretary and the painter Alonso Cano. Recent writers generally believe it is a self-portrait of the artist, though there is disagreement about the dating, some placing it as late as 1640. It is one of the most powerful of the portraits Velázquez painted after his return from Italy.

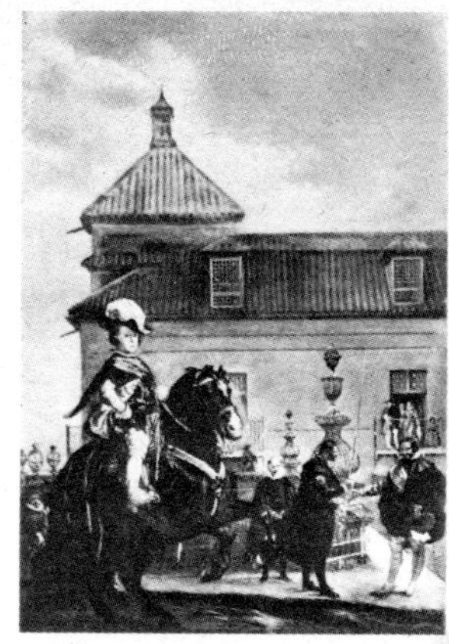
73

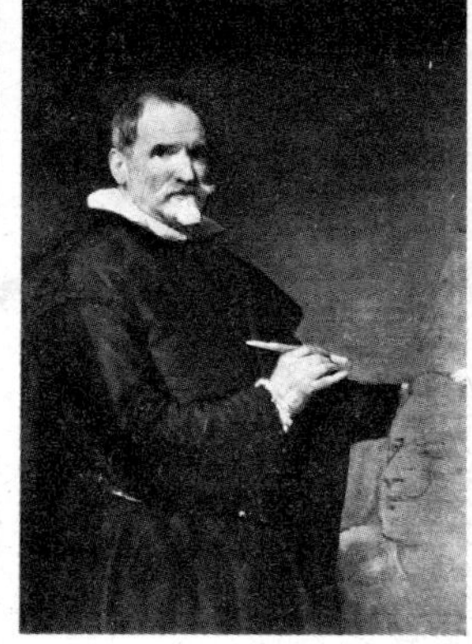
74

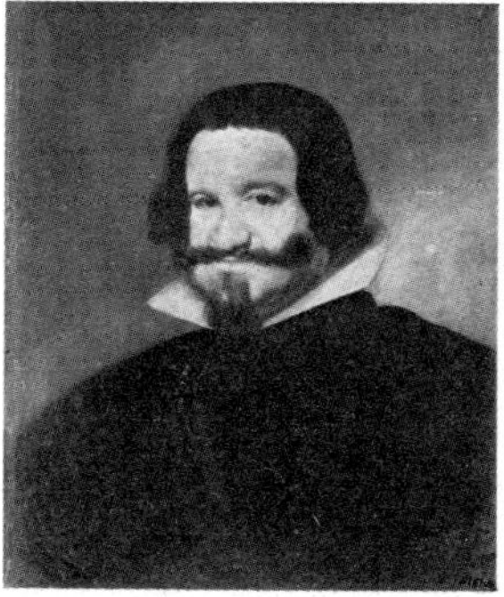
75

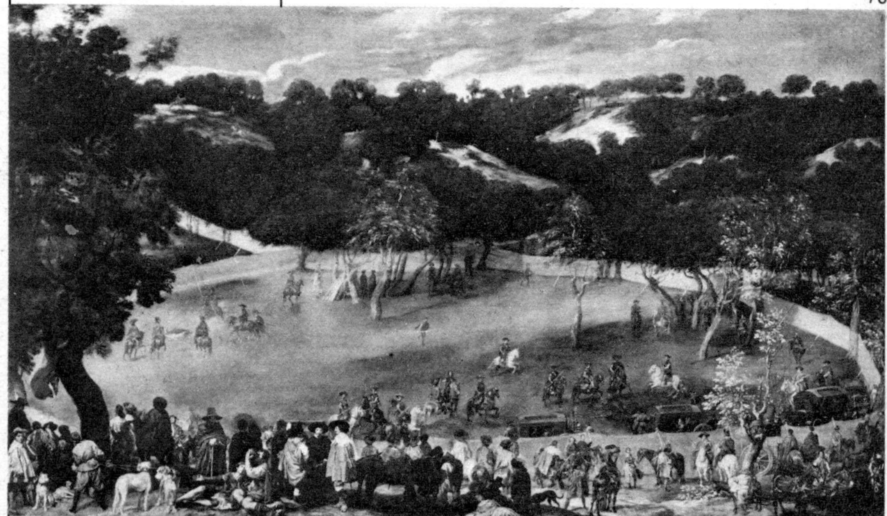
76

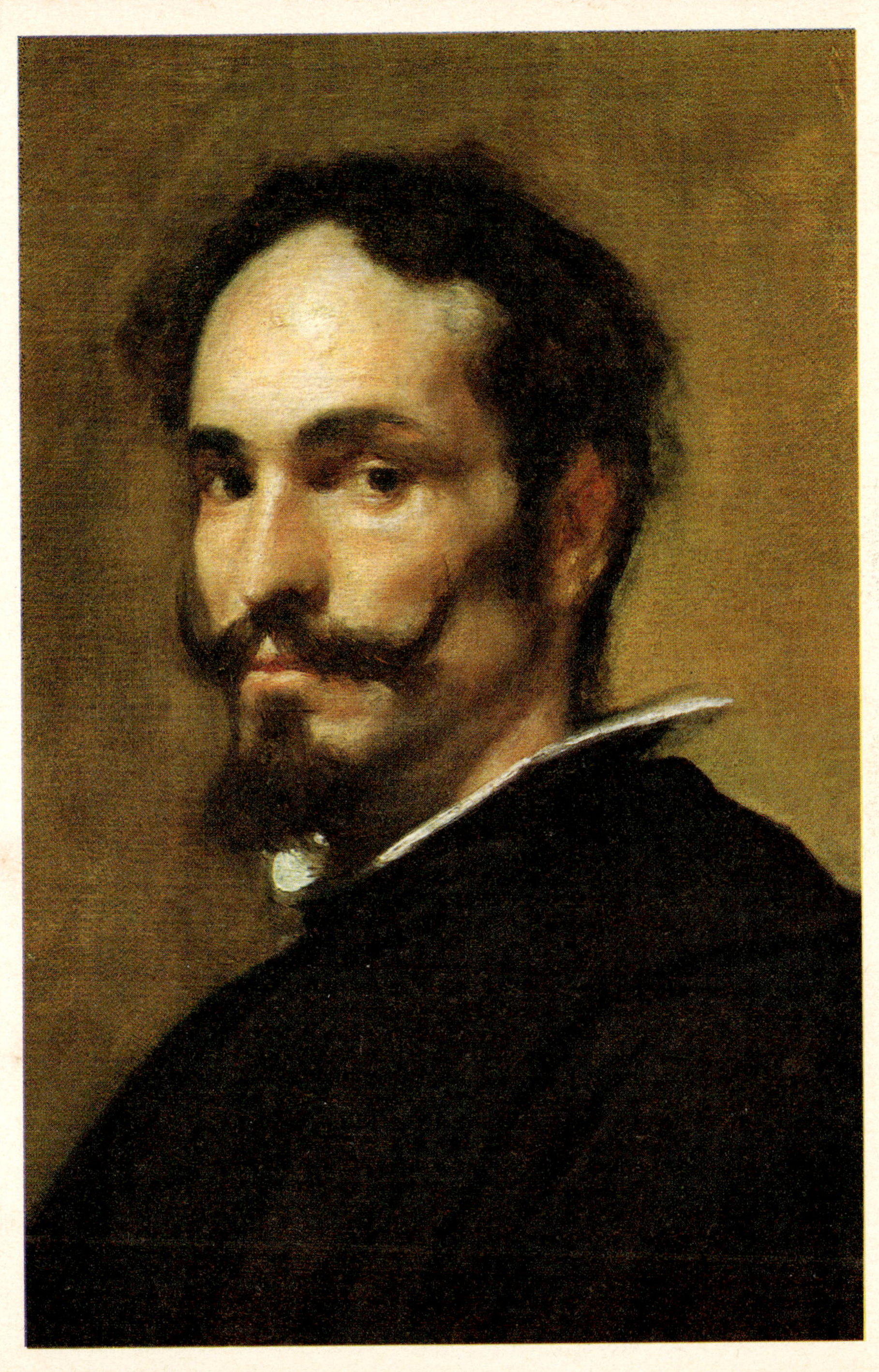

77 Portrait of a Bearded Man
Oil on canvas/76 × 64.5/
1638–40
London, Wellington Museum

78 Archbishop Fernando de Valdés y Llanos
Oil on canvas/68.5 × 59.6/
1639 (?)
London, National Gallery

79 Hand of an Ecclesiastic
Oil on canvas/68.5 × 59.6/
1639 (?)
Madrid, Palacio de Oriente
Fragment

80 Francesco II d'Este, Duke of Modena
Oil on canvas/68 × 51/1639
Modena, Pinacoteca Estense

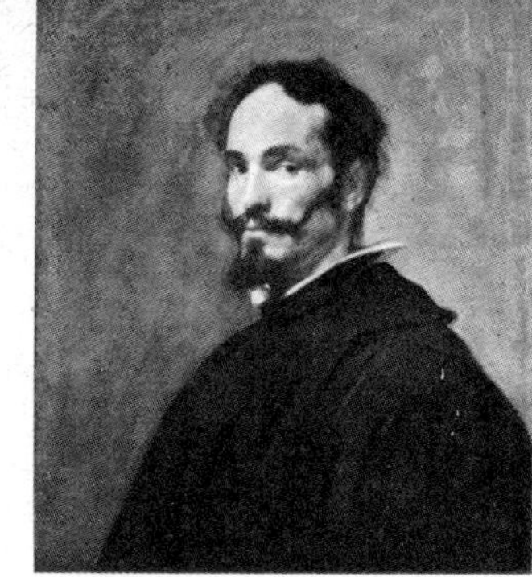

77

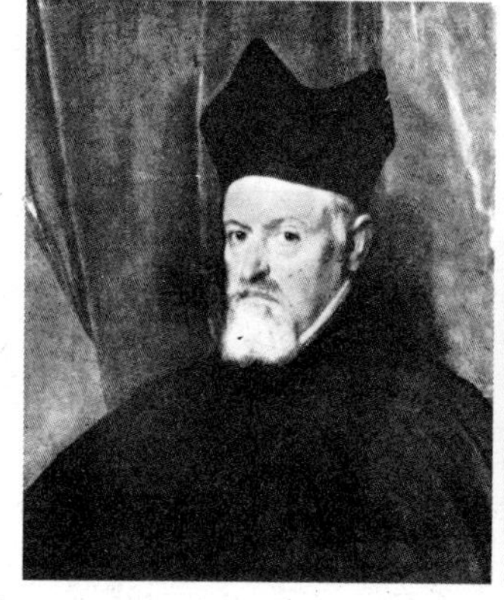

78

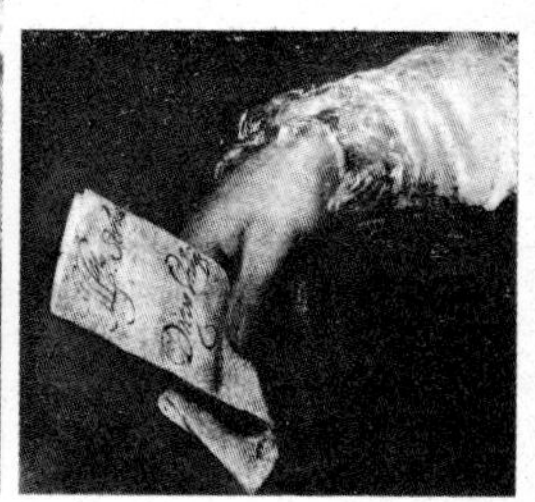

79

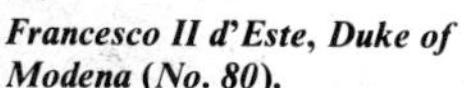

***Francesco II d'Este, Duke of Modena* (*No. 80*).**
According to Testi, the duke's minister in Madrid, Velázquez painted this portrait in March 1639 while the duke was on a visit to the court there. It is another outstanding example of Velázquez' extraordinary powers of synthesis in his work, increasingly apparent after his first visit to Italy.

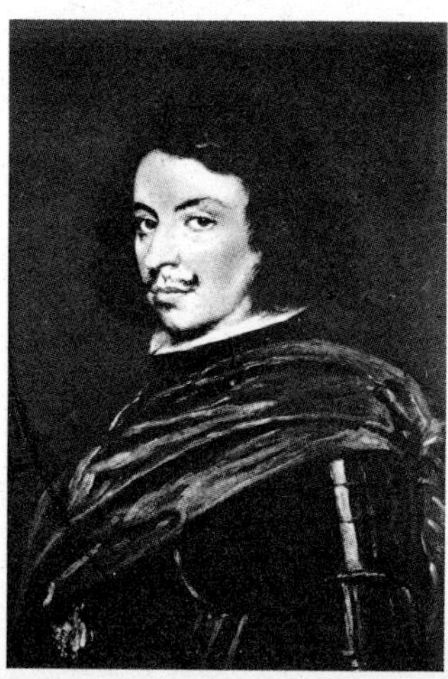

80

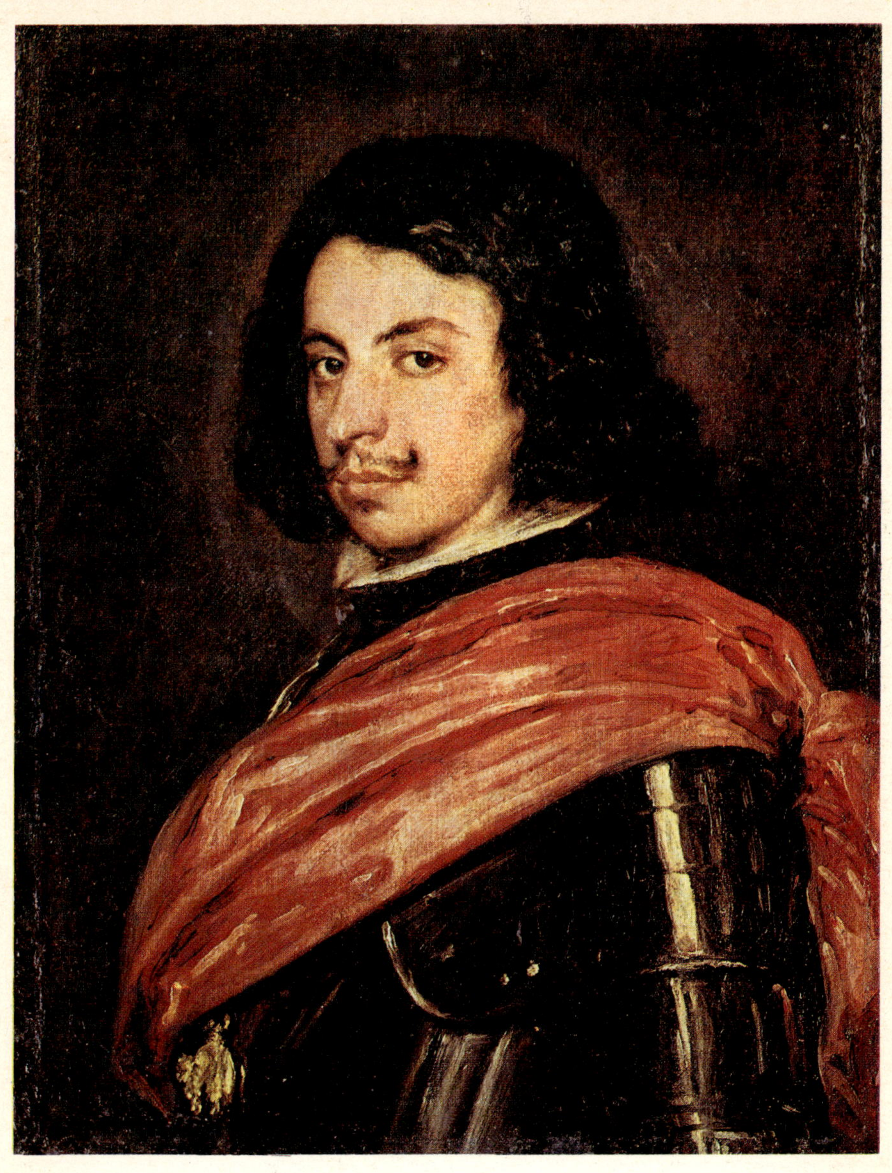

81 Calabazas
Oil on canvas/106 × 83/1639
Madrid, Prado

82 Prince Baltasar Carlos
Oil on canvas/128.5 × 99/
1639–40
Vienna, Kunsthistorisches
Museum

83 Menippus
Oil on canvas/179 × 94/
1639–40
Madrid, Prado

84 Aesop
Oil on canvas/179 × 94/
1639–40
Madrid, Prado

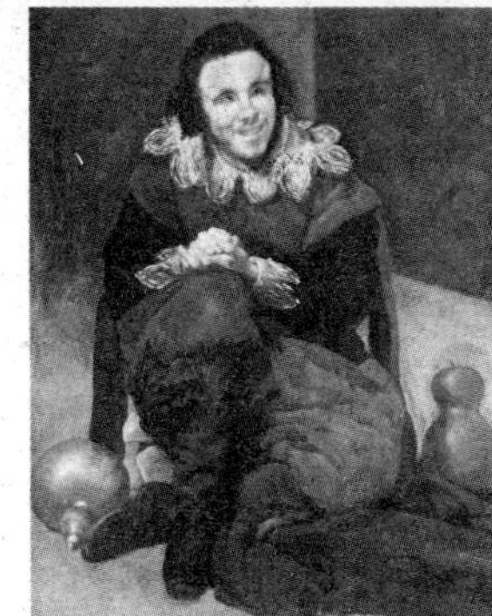

81

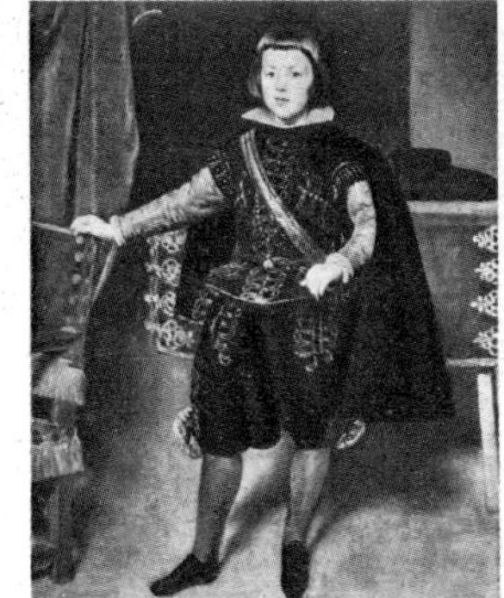

82

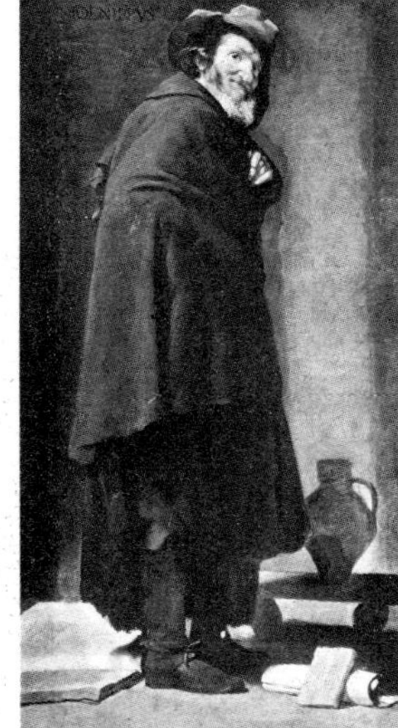

83

***Menippus* (*No. 83, detail*).**
A companion piece to the painting of Aesop (No. 84), also in the Prado. For his portraits of the two Greek philosophers Velázquez probably used models taken from everyday life and closely observed with a painter's eye to capture vividly their physical and mental qualities, presenting them as two men of the people made sadder and wiser by their experience of the world.

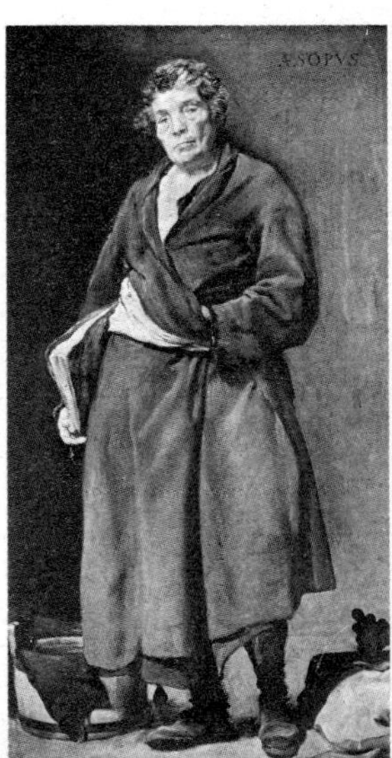

84

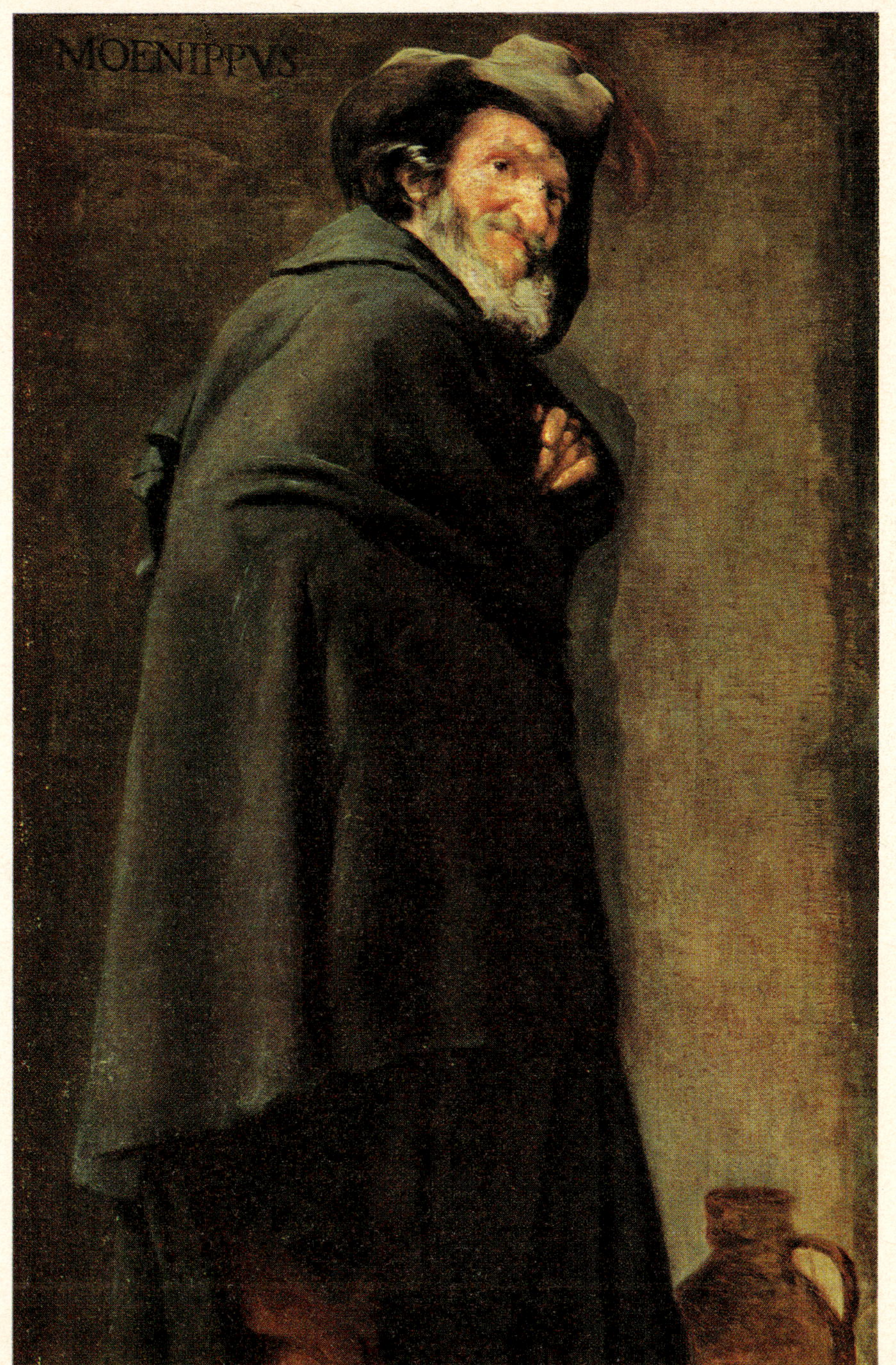
MOENIPPVS

85 Mars
Oil on canvas/179 × 95/
1640 (?)
Madrid, Prado

86 The Needlewoman
Oil on canvas/74 × 60/
1640 (?)
Washington, National
Gallery of Art

87 St Anthony Abbot and St Paul the Hermit
Oil on canvas/257 × 188/
1640 (?)
Madrid, Prado

Aesop (No. 84, detail).
This detail of the Greek philosopher's head shows how Velázquez successfully conveys the physical and human characteristics of his sitters simply by his swift economic brush strokes and use of densely applied colours and lights.

85

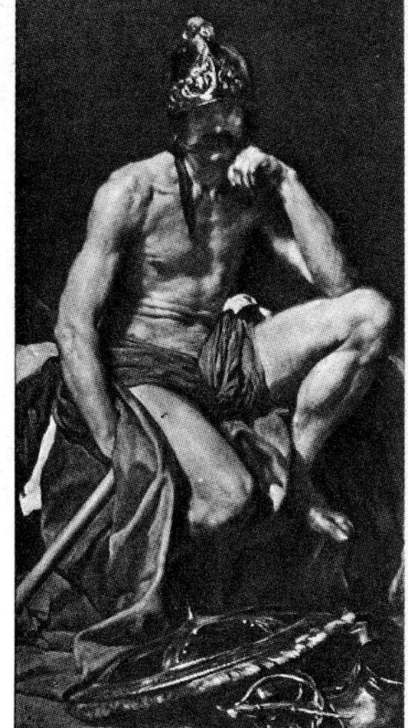

86

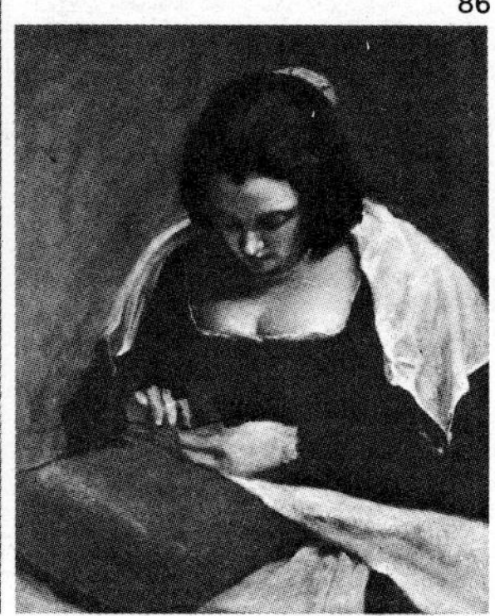

87

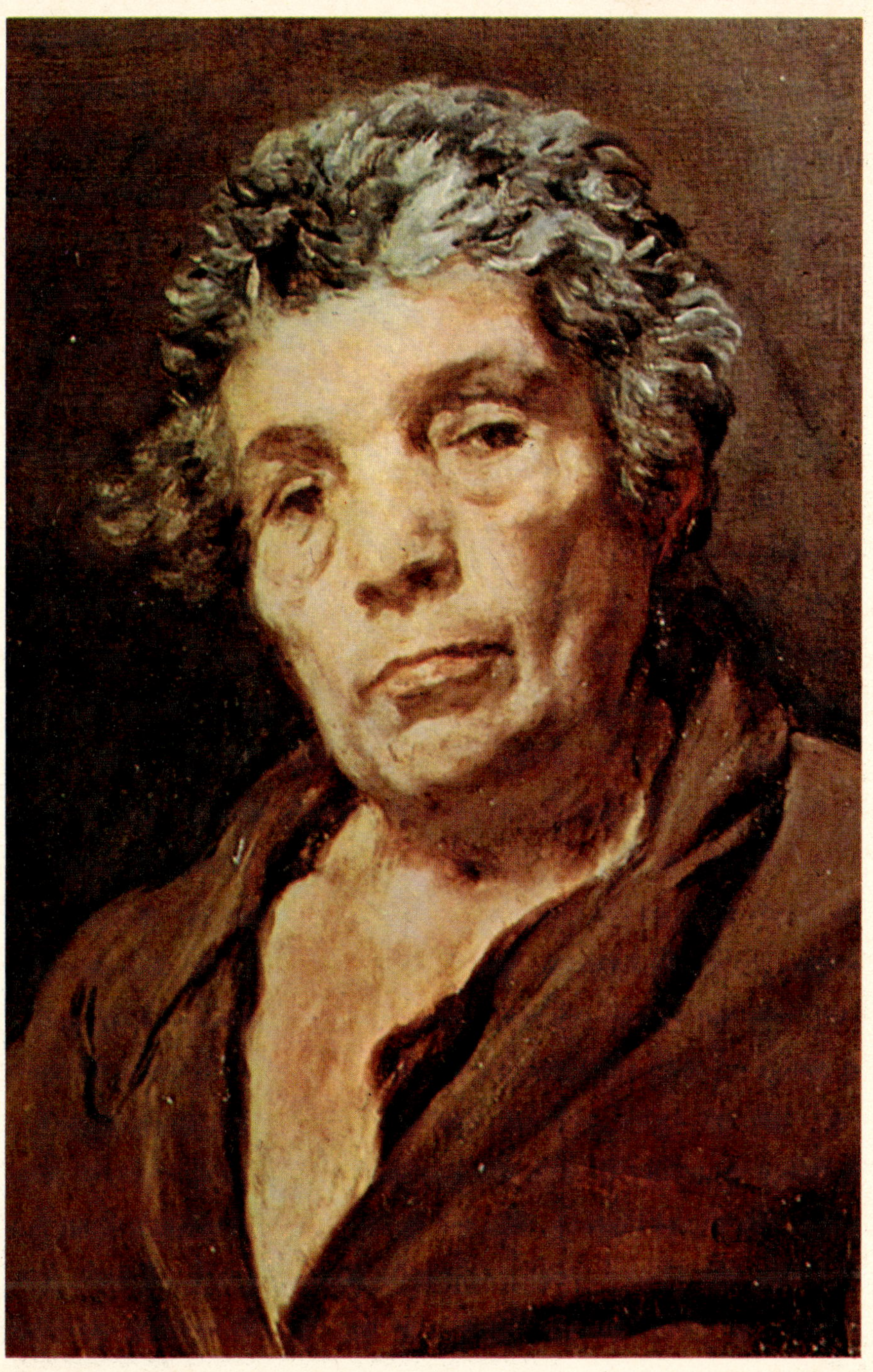

88 Lady with a Fan
Oil on canvas/93 × 68.5/
1640 (?)
London, Wallace Collection

89 Young Lady
Oil on canvas/71 × 47/
1640 (?)
Chatsworth, Duke of
Devonshire's Collection

90 Francisco Lezcano
Oil on canvas/107 × 83/
1640–2
Madrid, Prado

91 Self-portrait*
Oil on canvas/45.5 × 38/
1640–50
Valencia, Museo Provincial

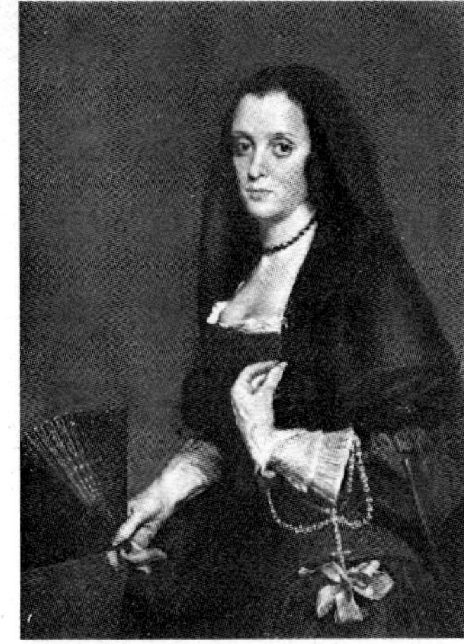

88

89

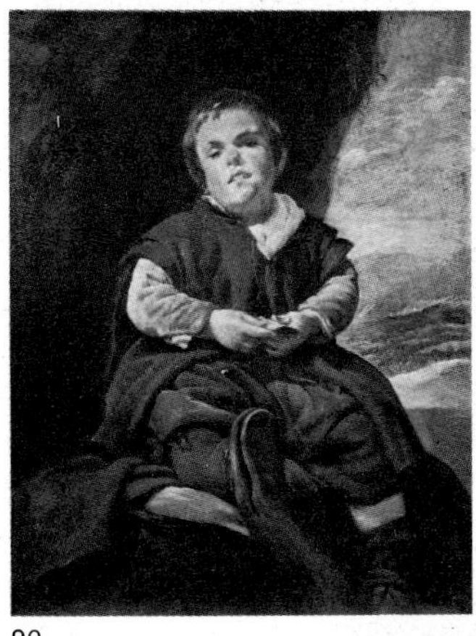

90

The Needlewoman (*No. 86*).
Some scholars have identified this as a portrait of Velázquez' daughter Francisca, wife of the painter Juan Bautista del Mazo. The quality of light and the pictorial synthesis of formal elements leave no doubt about the work's authenticity, sometimes questioned. This intimate and perceptive portrayal of a homely scene from domestic life is certainly one of Velázquez' most remarkable works.

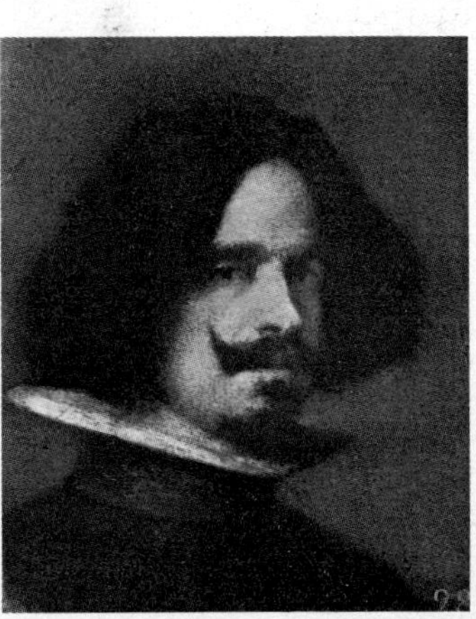

91

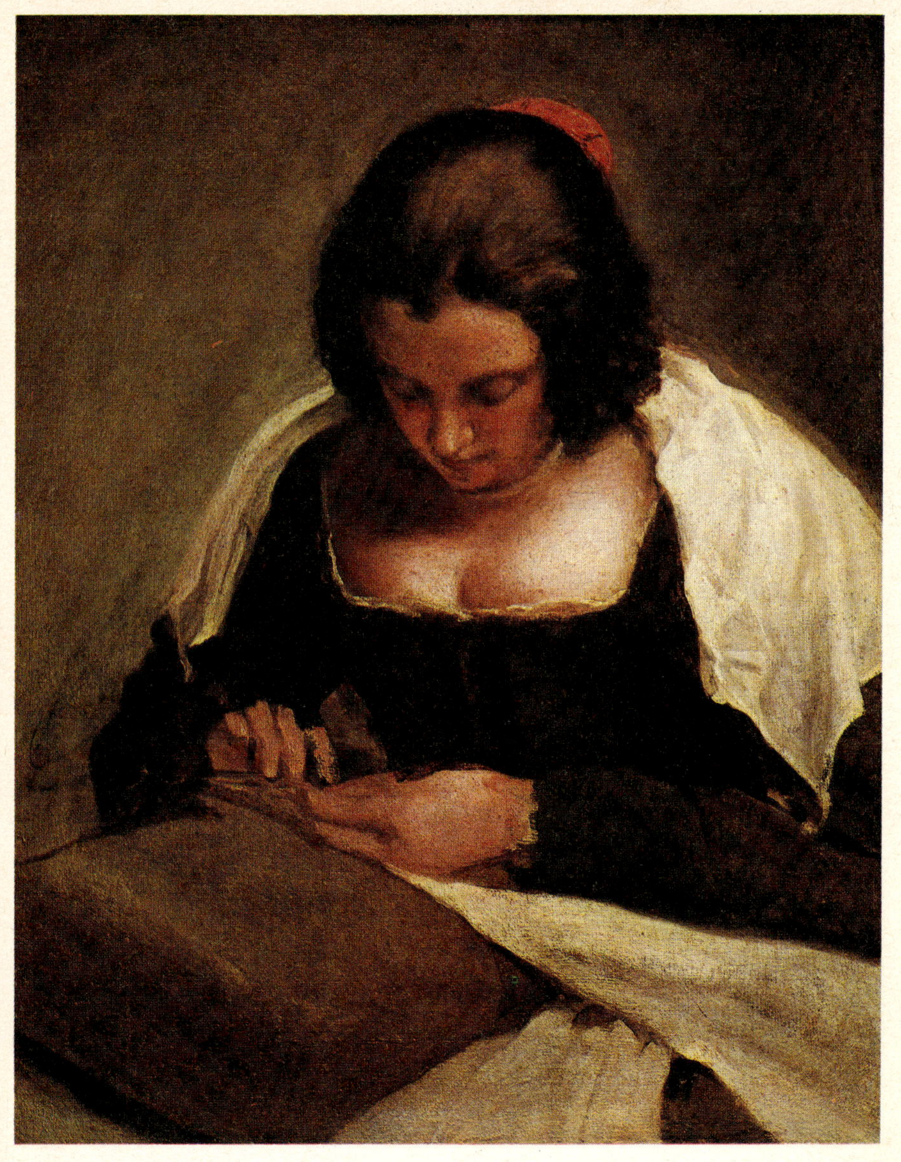

92 Portrait of a Cleric
Oil on canvas/66.5 × 51/1623 or 1640
Madrid, Payá Collection

93 The Coronation of the Virgin
Oil on canvas/176 × 134/ 1641–2
Madrid, Prado

94 Portrait of a Girl
Oil on canvas/51.5 × 41/ 1642 (?)
New York, Hispanic Society of America

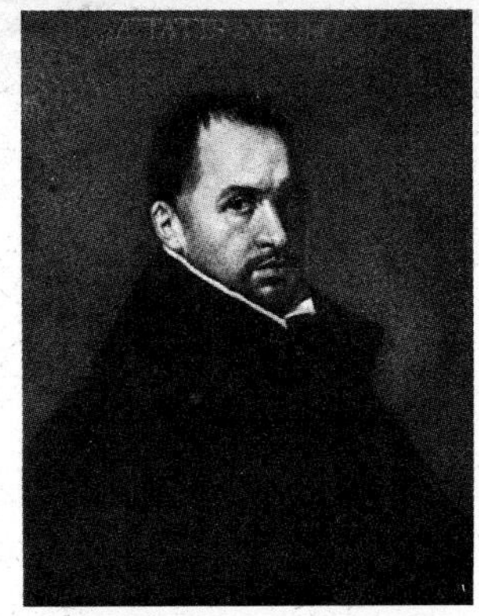

92

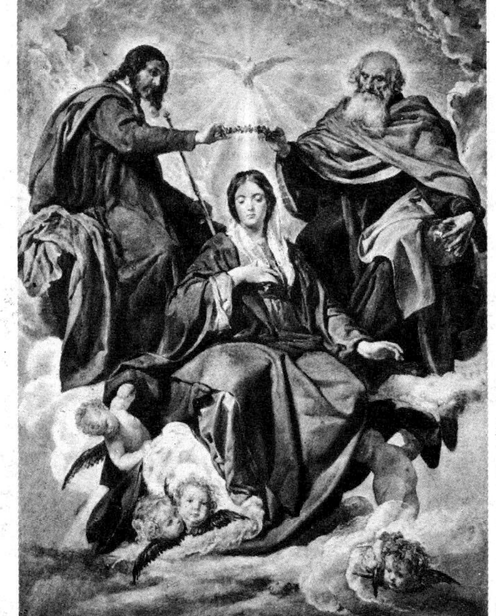

93

St Anthony Abbot and St Paul the Hermit (No. 87). *This canvas shows several episodes from the lives of the two saints, a common device of medieval iconography. However, here as nowhere else Velázquez treats his religious theme as a pretext for creating one of the finest landscapes of seventeenth-century painting. Echoes of landscape views by Dürer or Patinir are transformed by Velázquez' powerful pictorial imagination.*

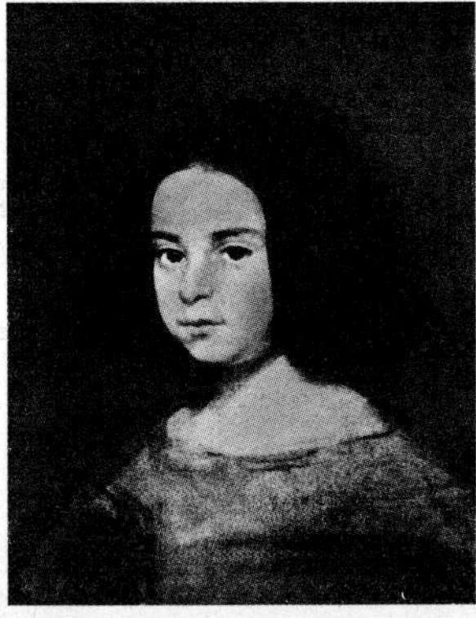

94

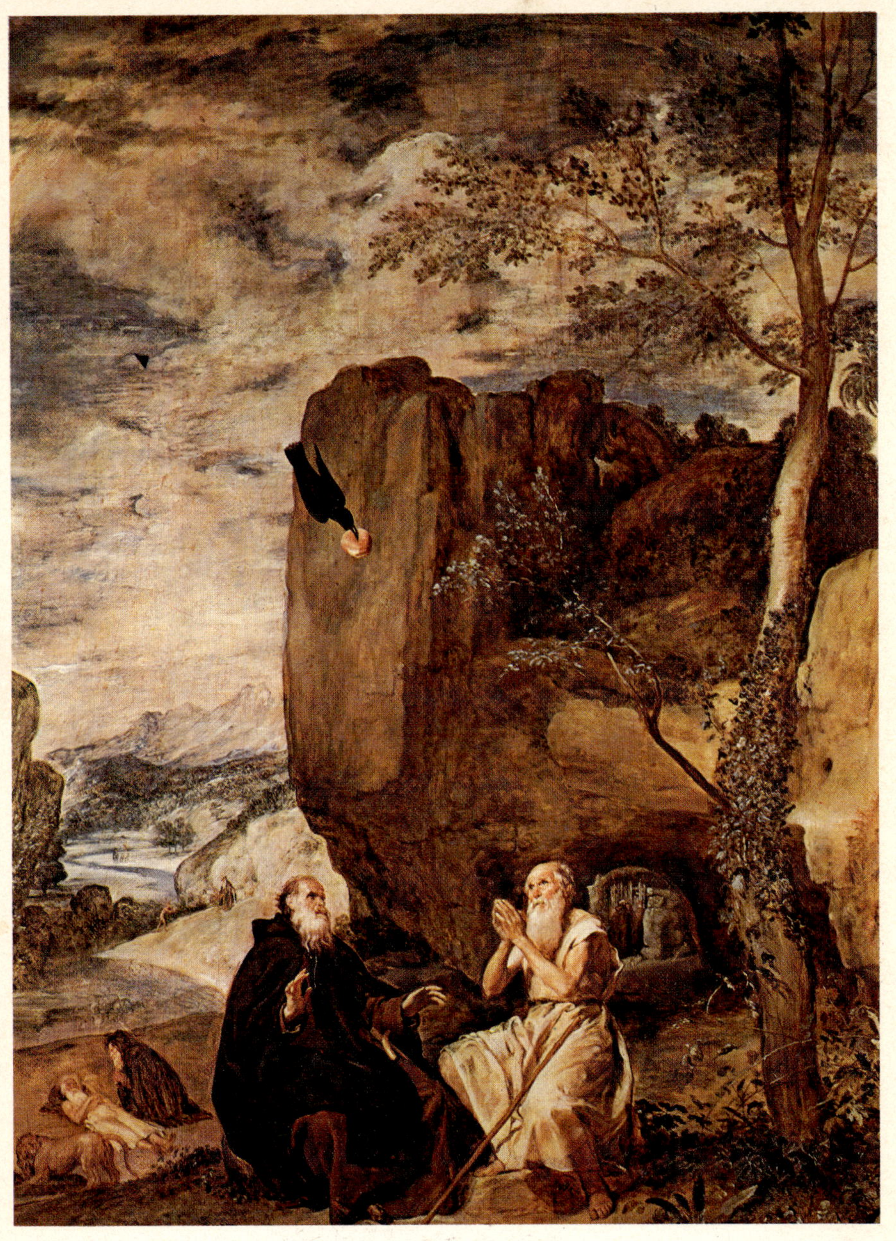

95 Don Juan de Austria
Oil on canvas/210 × 123/ 1643 (?)
Madrid, Prado

96 Cardinal Borgia
Oil on canvas pasted on board/47.5 × 40/1643–5
Wimborne, Dorset, Bankes Collection

97 Philip IV in Army Dress (the Fraga portrait)
Oil on canvas/133 × 98.5/1644
New York, Frick Collection

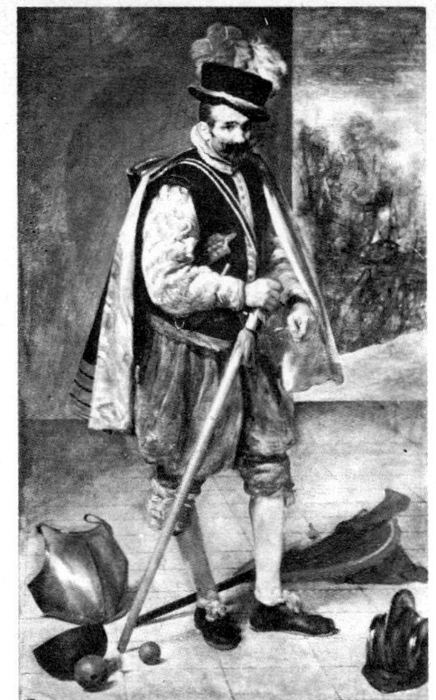

95

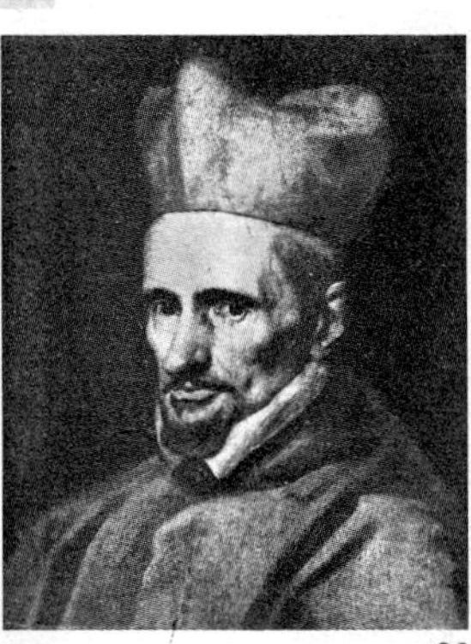

96

Lady with a Fan (No. 88).
A marvellous portrait, possibly of Velázquez' daughter. Justi sees the lady as 'a maze of coldness and fire, of bigotry and worldliness, of pride and coquetry or worse'. Variously thought to have been painted soon after 1630 or more probably in the 1640s. There is a variant of the painting, possibly autograph, at Chatsworth (No. 89).

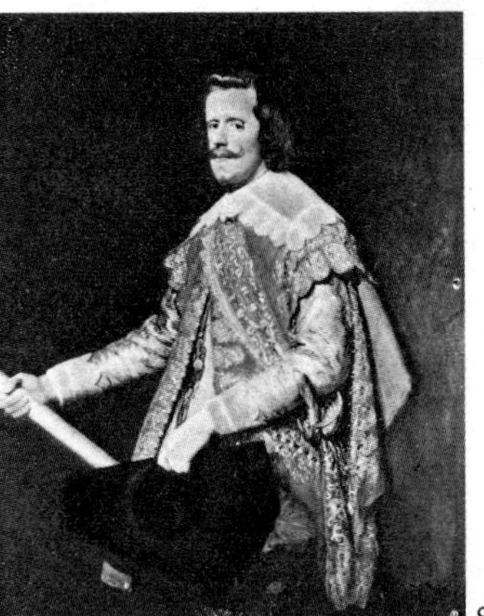

97

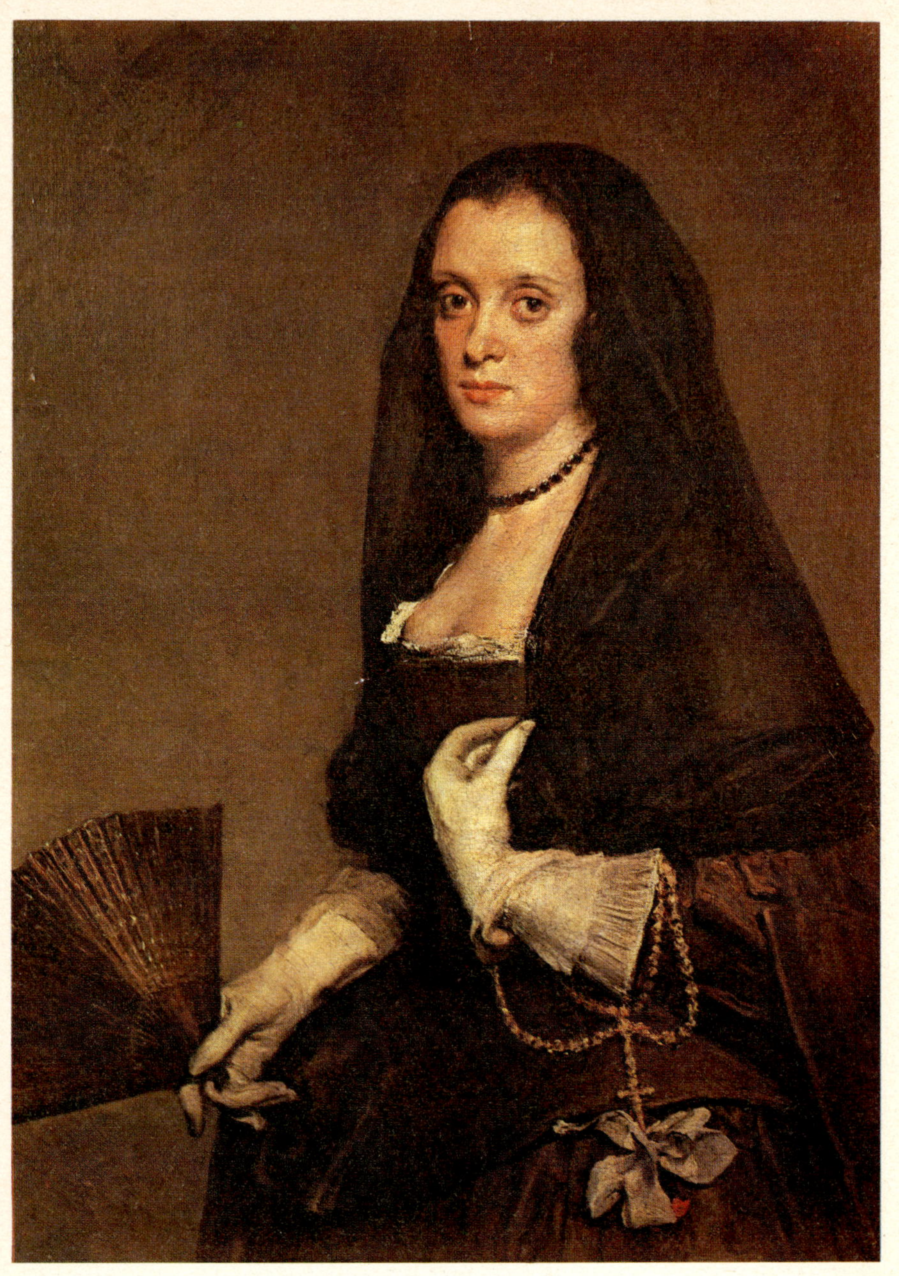

98 Don Diego de Acedo, 'El Primo'
Oil on canvas/107 × 82/1644
Madrid, Prado

99 Sebastián de Morra
Oil on canvas/106 × 81/1644
Madrid, Prado

100 A Knight of Santiago
Oil on canvas/66.5 × 56/1645–8
Dresden, Gemäldegalerie

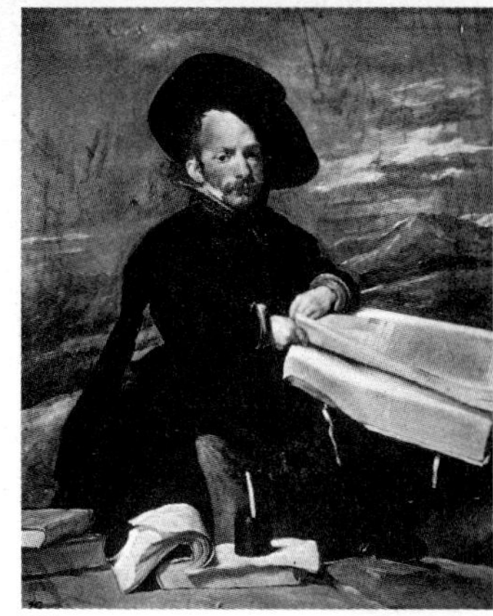

98

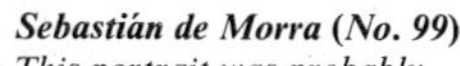

***Sebastián de Morra* (*No. 99*).** *This portrait was probably originally one of a series of court jesters painted at different times which, on grounds of similarity of composition and form, seems to have included the portraits of* Francisco Lezcano *(*El Niño de Vallecas, *No. 90),* Calabazas *(No. 81) and* Don Diego de Acedo, 'El Primo' *(No. 98), now all in the Prado.* Sebastián de Morra *probably dates from the same period as* 'El Primo'*, painted at Fraga in 1644.*

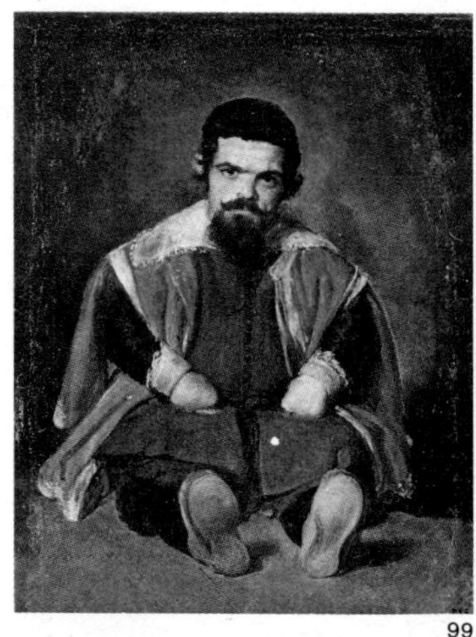

99

***Venus at her Mirror* (*No. 106*)** (pp. 70–71). *Painted almost certainly during Velázquez' second visit to Italy, this is one of the very few female nudes by him but one of the most famous in the whole of European art. A marvellous image of a woman, with extraordinary delicacy of light and colour, it belongs to the tradition of female nudes which began with Titian, and anticipates similar interpretations by Goya, Manet and above all Renoir.*

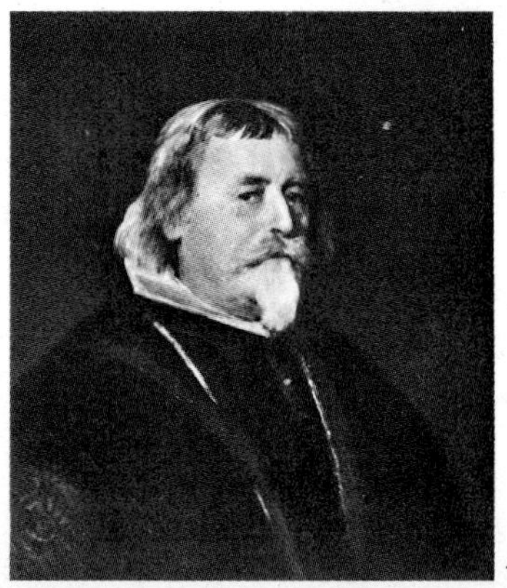

100

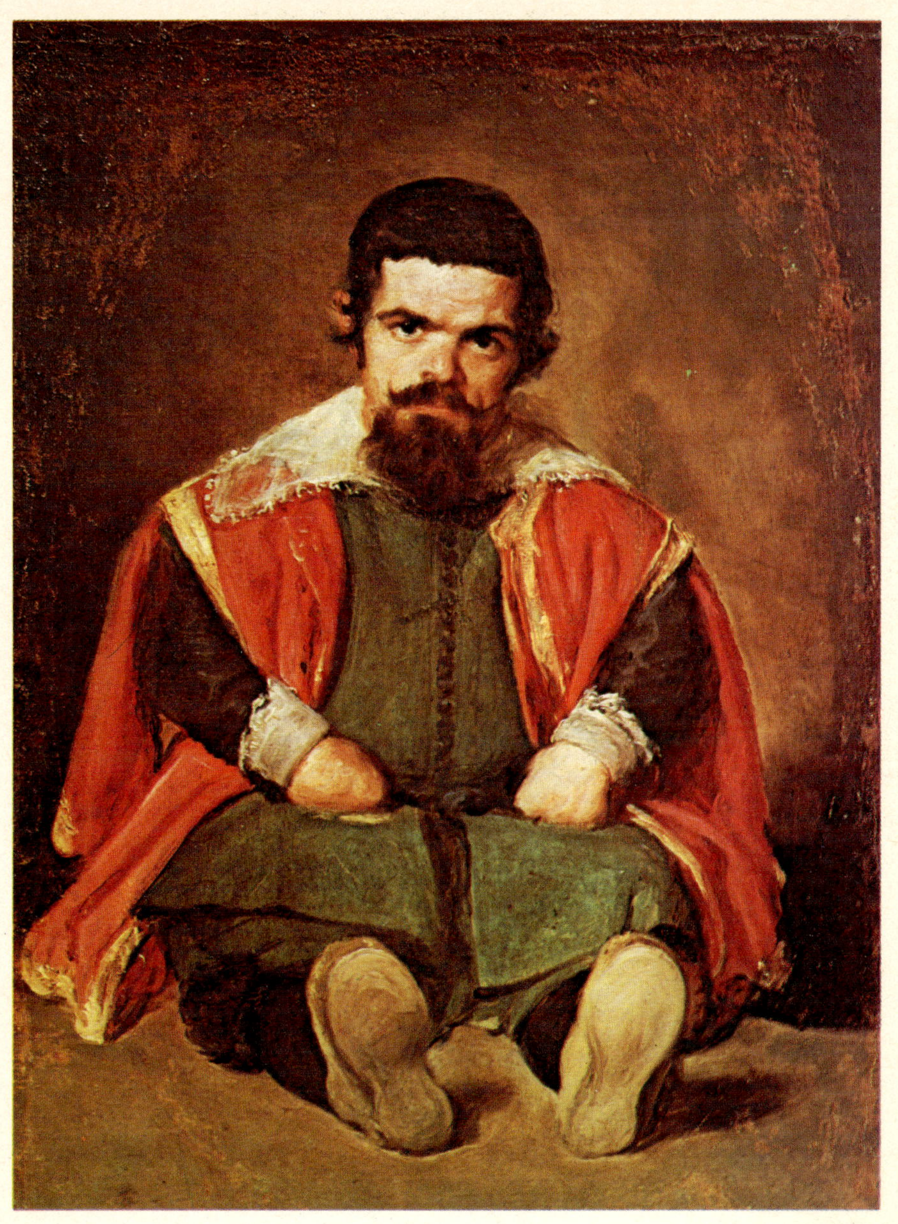

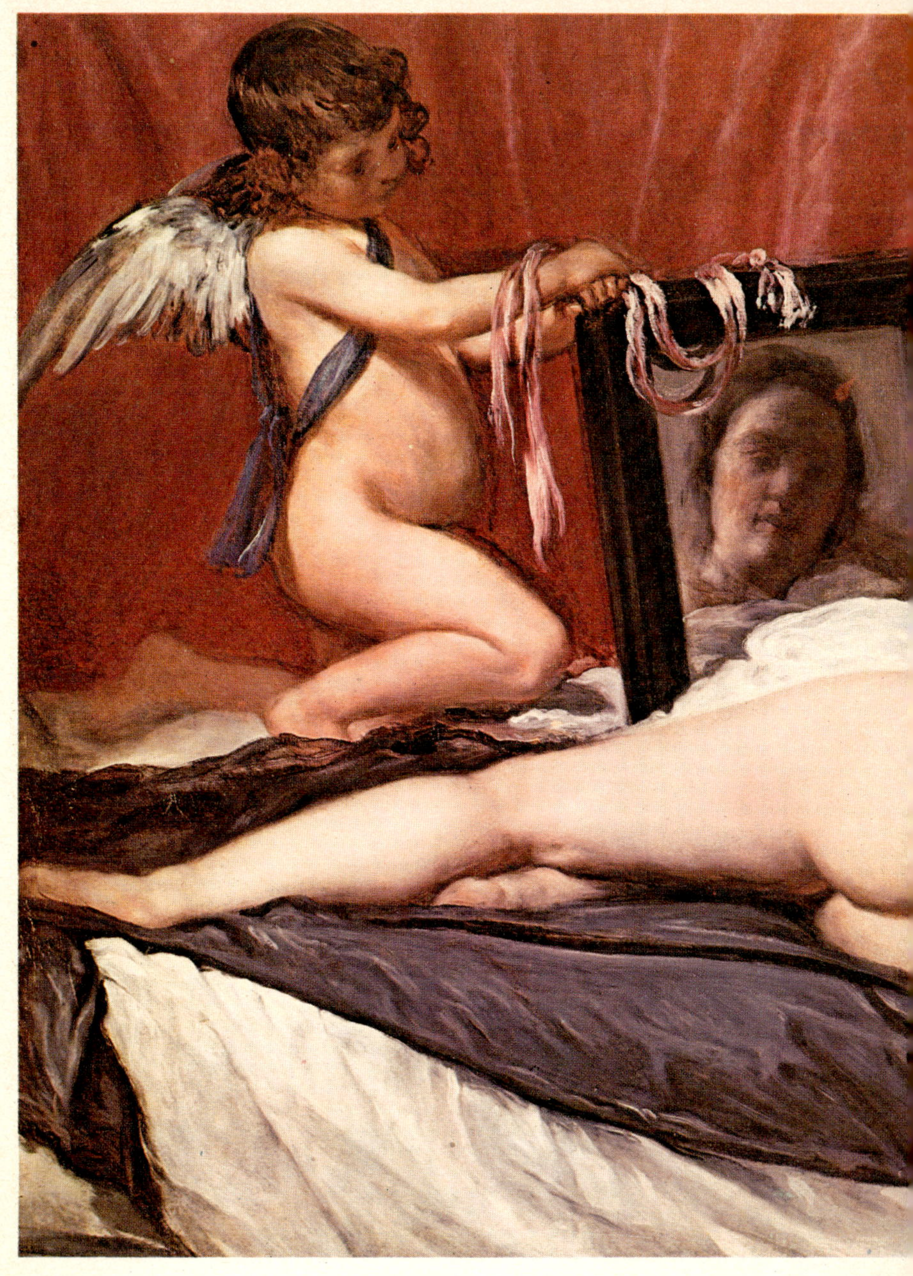

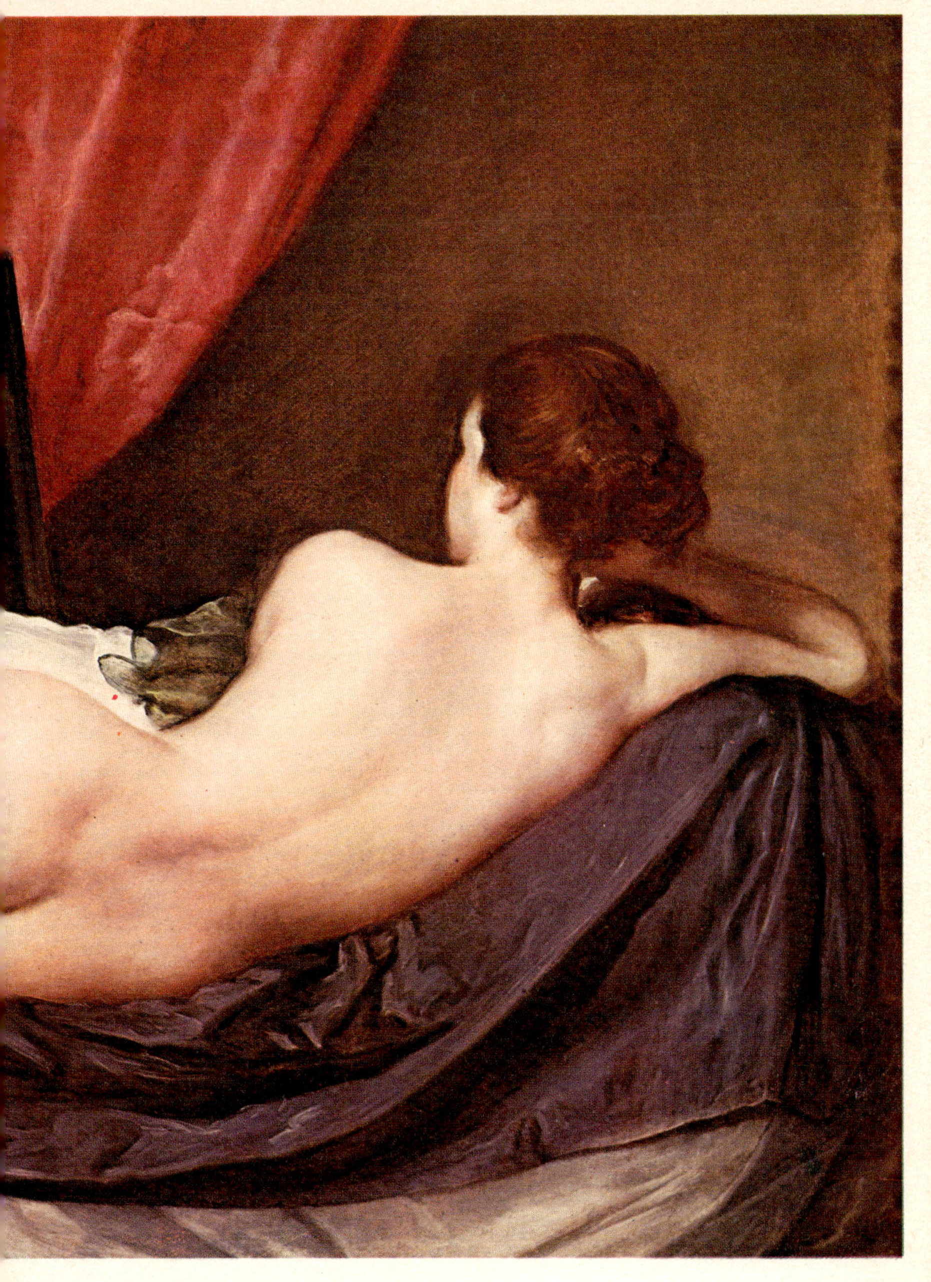

101 View of Saragossa
Oil on canvas/181 × 331/1647
Madrid, Prado
(with the collaboration of Mazo)

102 Conde de Benavente
Oil on canvas/109 × 88/1648
Madrid, Prado

103 Portrait of an Elderly Man
Oil on canvas/65 × 44/1648
New York, Art Market

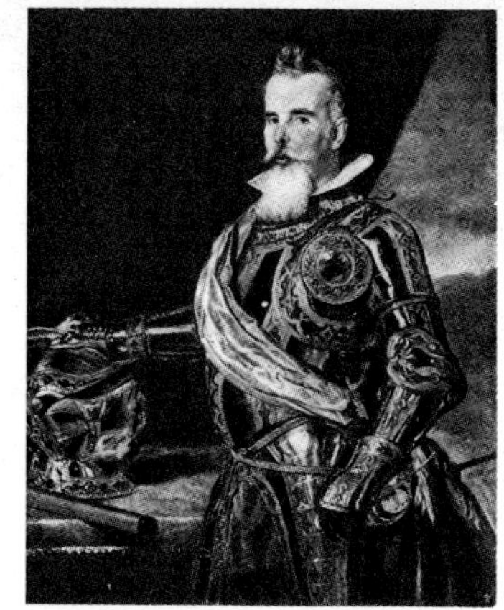
102

Villa Medici in Rome (No. 109).
This painting and its companion piece of the Villa Medici with the statue of the sleeping Ariadne (No. 110), the first shown in a strong noon light, the second in the warm, sensual glow of evening, are among the finest of Velázquez' mature landscapes, foreshadowing the nineteenth-century approach of Corot and later the Impressionists.

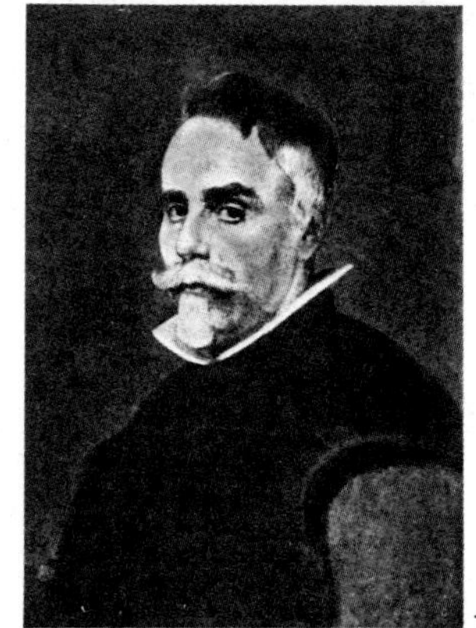
103

101
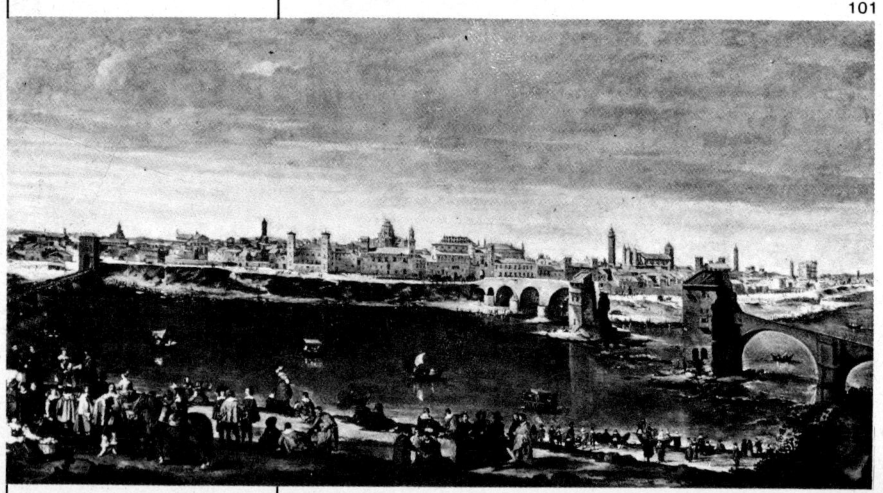

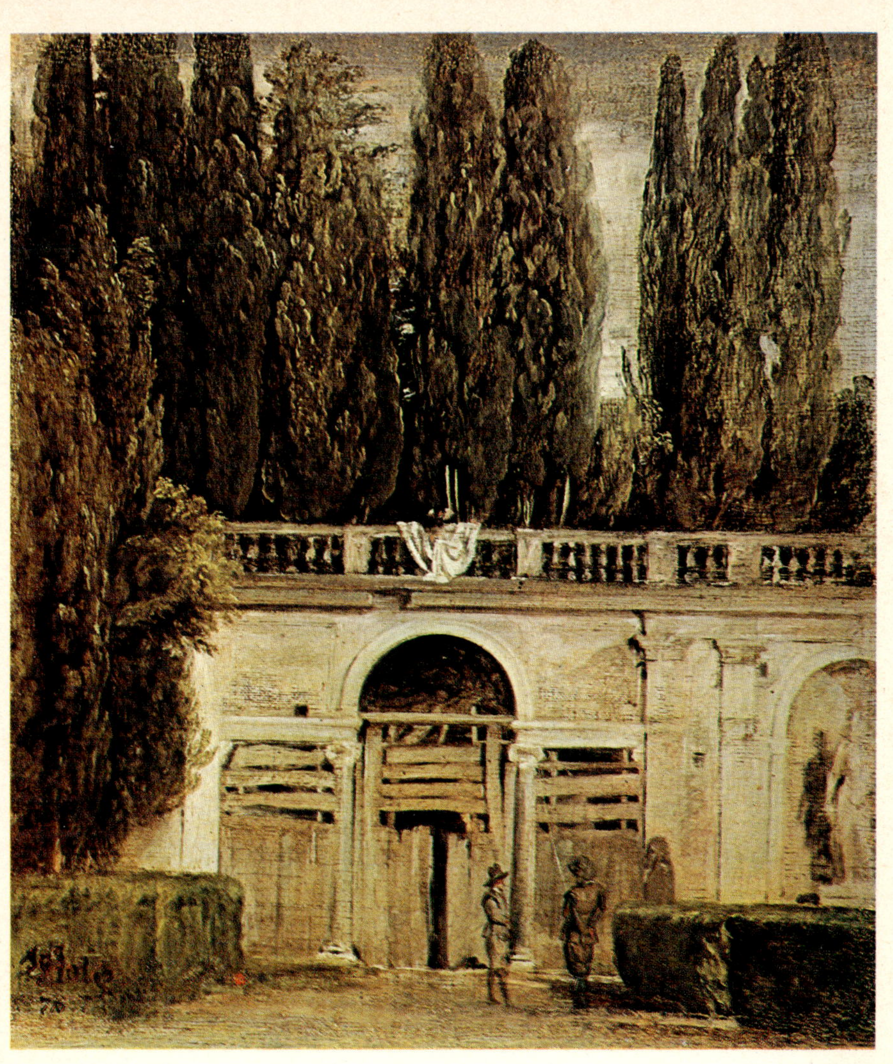

104 The Infanta María Teresa
Oil on canvas/48 × 37/1648
New York, Lehman Collection

105 A Woman as a Sibyl
Oil on canvas/64 × 58/1648–50
New York, Private Collection

106 Venus at her Mirror
Oil on canvas/122 × 177/1648–50
London, National Gallery

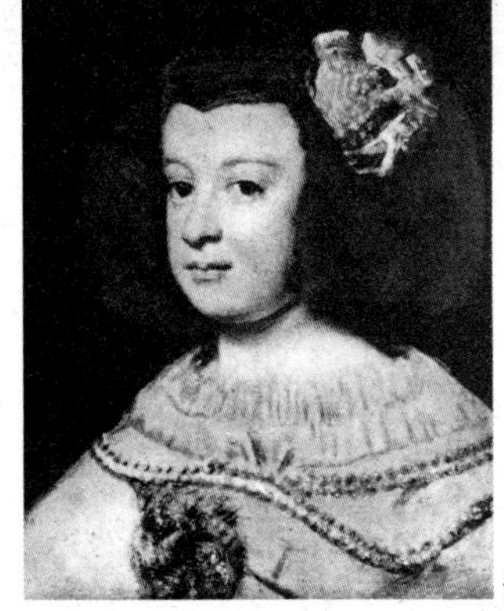
104

***Juan de Pareja* (*No. 112*).** *A portrait of Velázquez' Morisco assistant who accompanied the artist on his second visit to Italy. Painted in Rome in 1650, it was then exhibited with great success in the Pantheon. Though not in a perfect state of preservation it is certainly one of the finest of Velázquez' mature works and deserved the acclaim it received in Rome.*

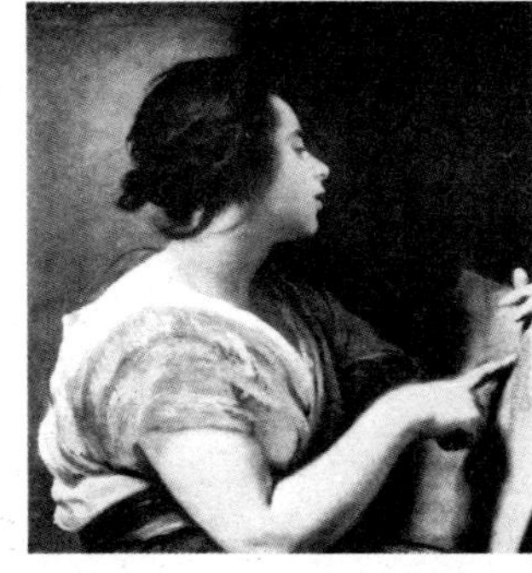
105

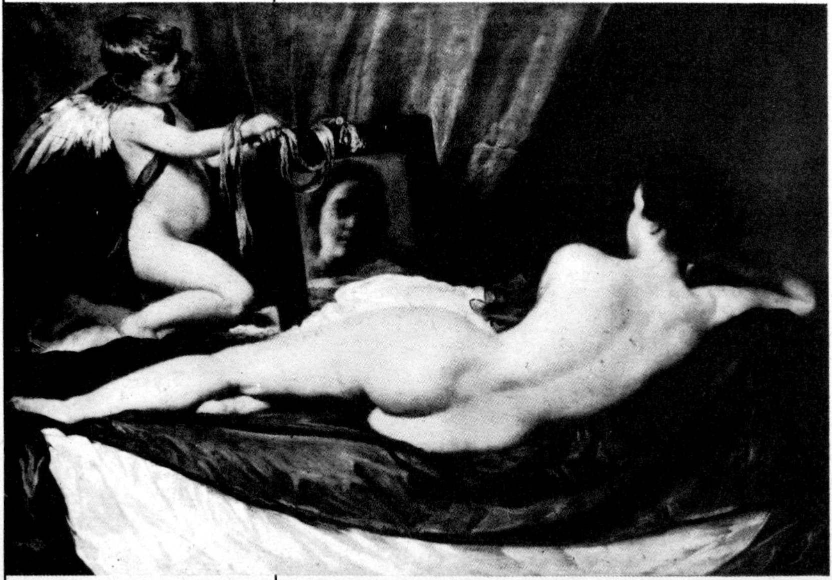

106

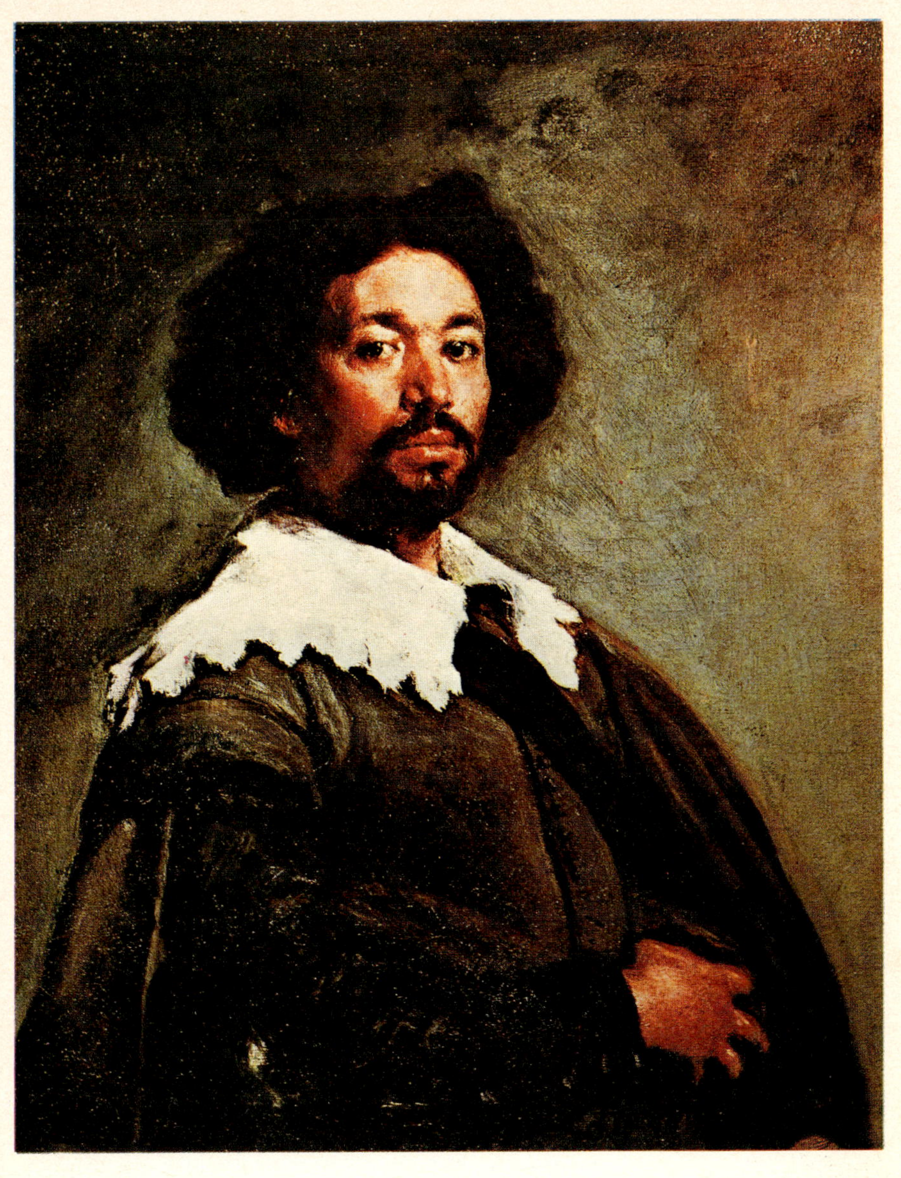

107 Monsignor Camillo Massimi
Oil on canvas/74 × 58.5/1650
New York, Metropolitan Museum of Art

108 Barber to the Pope
Oil on canvas/48.3 × 44.4/1650
New York, Private Collection

109 Villa Medici in Rome
Oil on canvas/48 × 42/1650 or 1630
Madrid, Prado

107

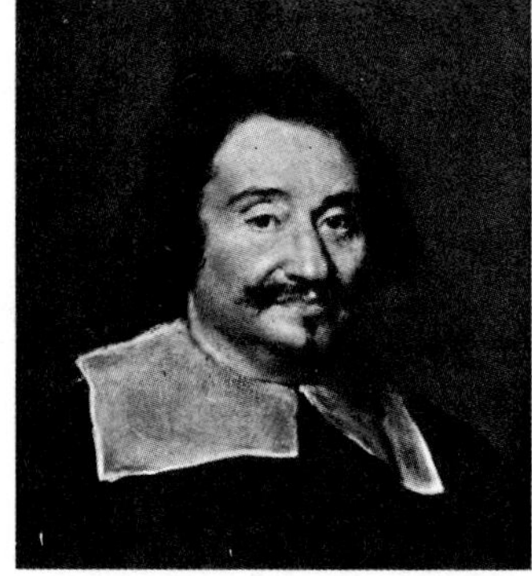

108

***Pope Innocent X* (*No. 113*).** *One of Velázquez' most famous portraits, an outstanding example of the limits to which he took the lessons he had learned from Titian's warm use of colour. He achieves extraordinary juxtapositions of colour (the different reds of the background hanging, the velvet armchair, the Pope's* biretta, *face and silk cape, the silvery-white of his alb and the gold decorations on the chair), harmonized by skilful use of light and freely applied paint.*

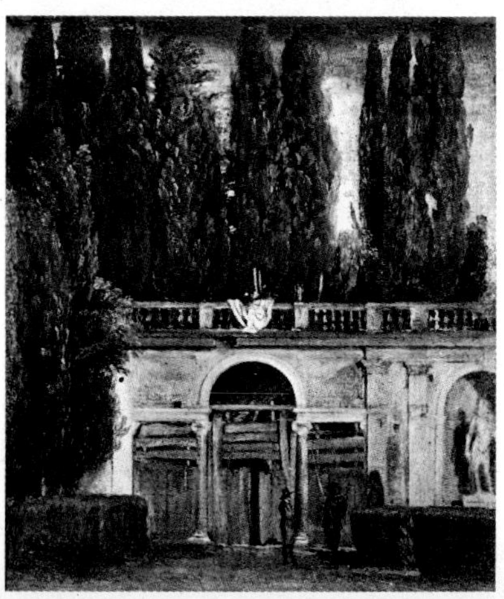

109

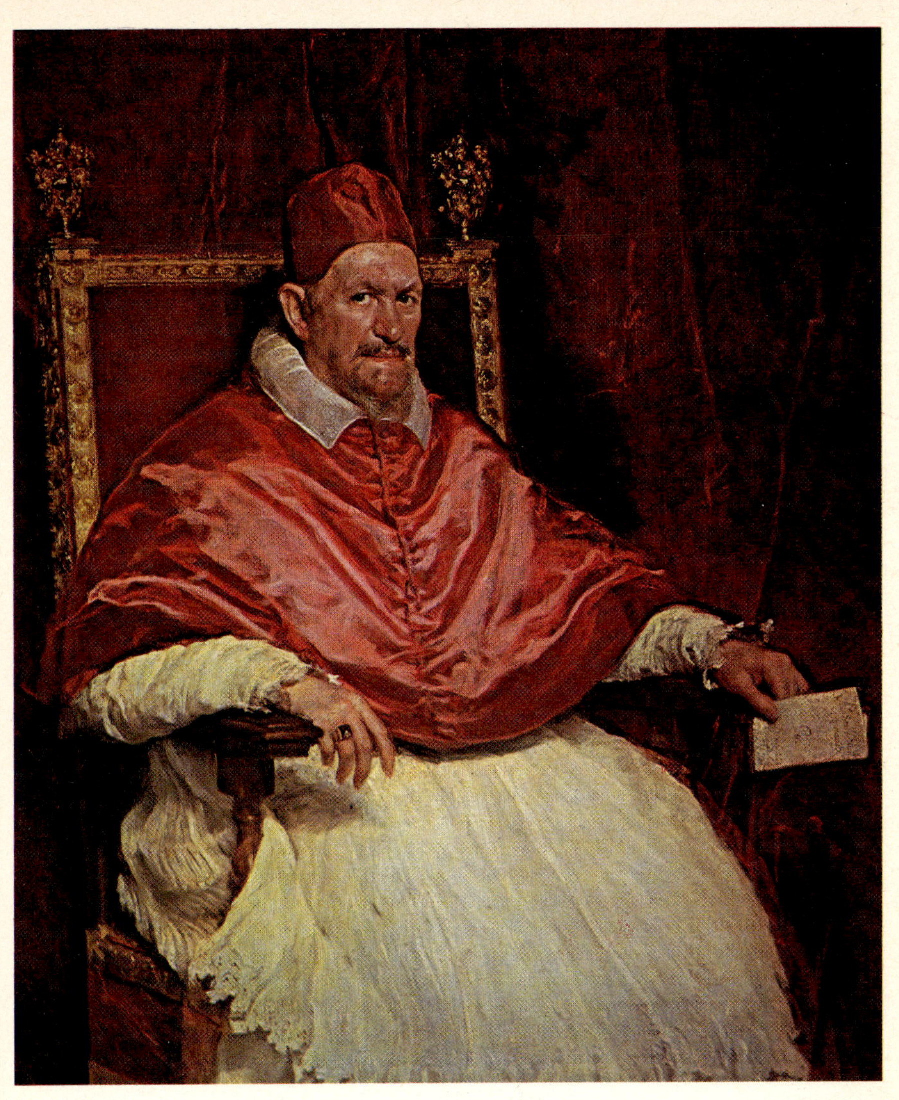

110 Villa Medici in Rome (with the statue of the sleeping Ariadne)
Oil on canvas/44 × 38/1650 or 1630
Madrid, Prado

111 Cardinal Astalli
Oil on canvas/61 × 48.5/1650 (?)
New York, Hispanic Society of America

112 Juan de Pareja
Oil on canvas/77.4 × 64/1650
New York, Metropolitan Museum of Art

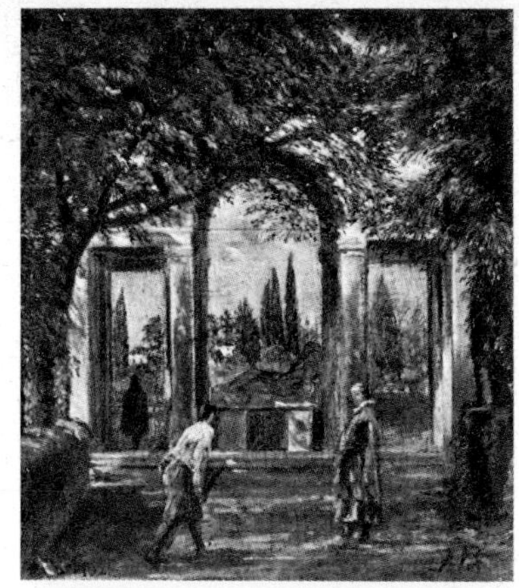

110

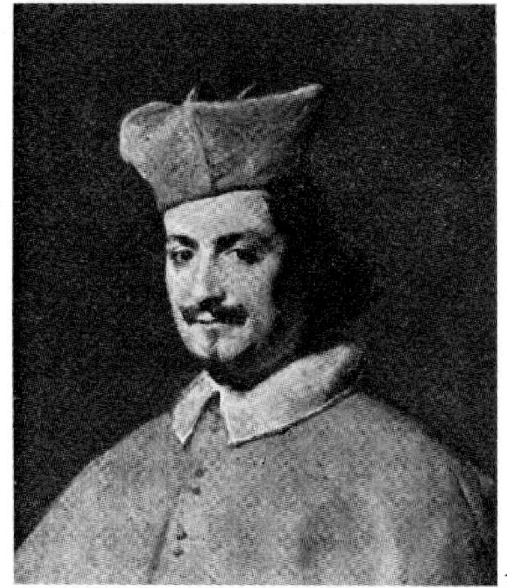

111

The Infanta Margarita (*No. 122*).
Velázquez painted a number of portraits of the Infanta Margarita, daughter of Philip IV and Queen Mariana of Austria, who was born in 1651 and married Leopold I of Germany in 1666. In the Vienna portrait the little princess is the same age and wears the same dress as in The Maids of Honour *and she is standing in the same way. This suggests not only that both works were painted in the same year (1656), but that the portrait may actually, according to some scholars, have been a preparatory study for the larger work.*

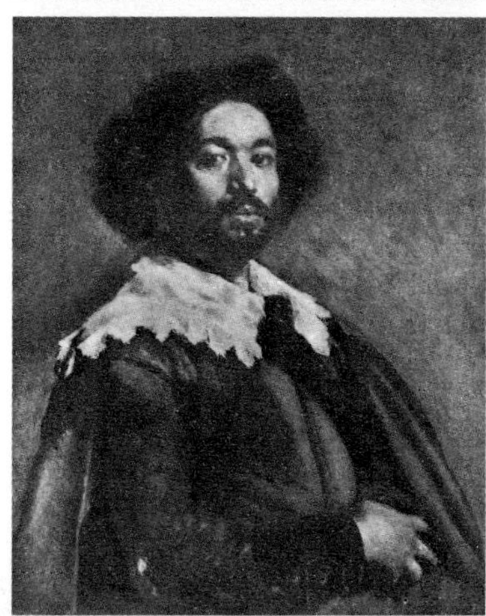

112

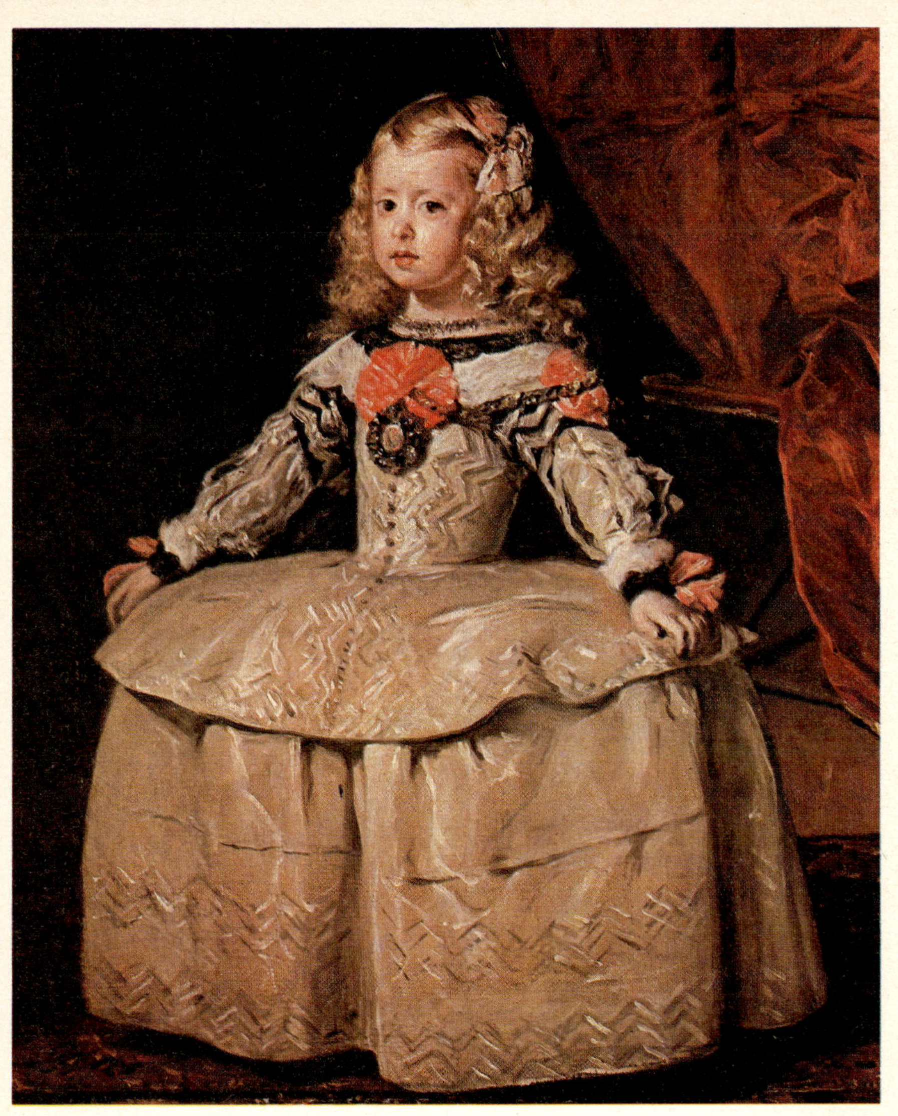

113 Pope Innocent X
Oil on canvas/140 × 120/
s. 1650
Rome, Galleria Doria
Pamphili

114 Pope Innocent X
Oil on canvas/78 × 68/1650
London, Wellington Museum

115 The Infanta María Teresa
Oil on canvas/44.5 × 40/
1651 (?)
New York, Metropolitan
Museum of Art

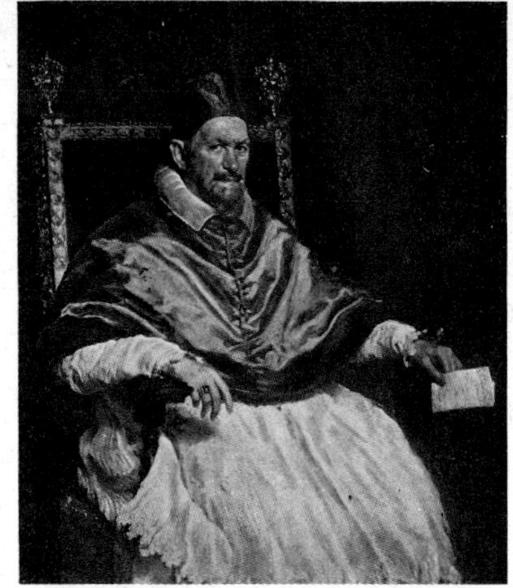

113

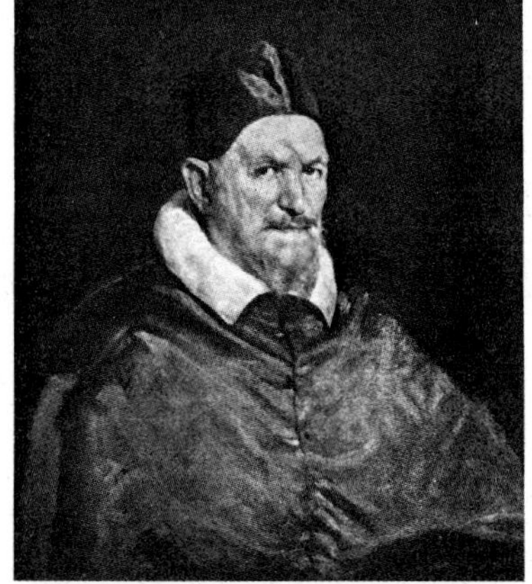

114

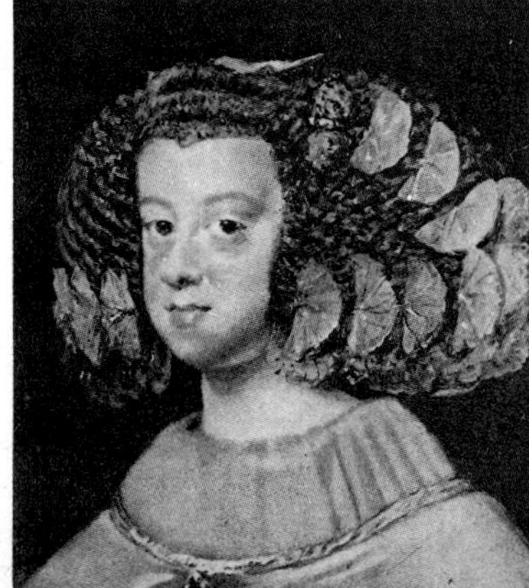

115

The Maids of Honour
(No. 123, detail).
A portrait of the artist himself engaged in painting the Spanish king and queen. Velázquez added the cross of the Order of Santiago on his doublet after 1659 when he received it.

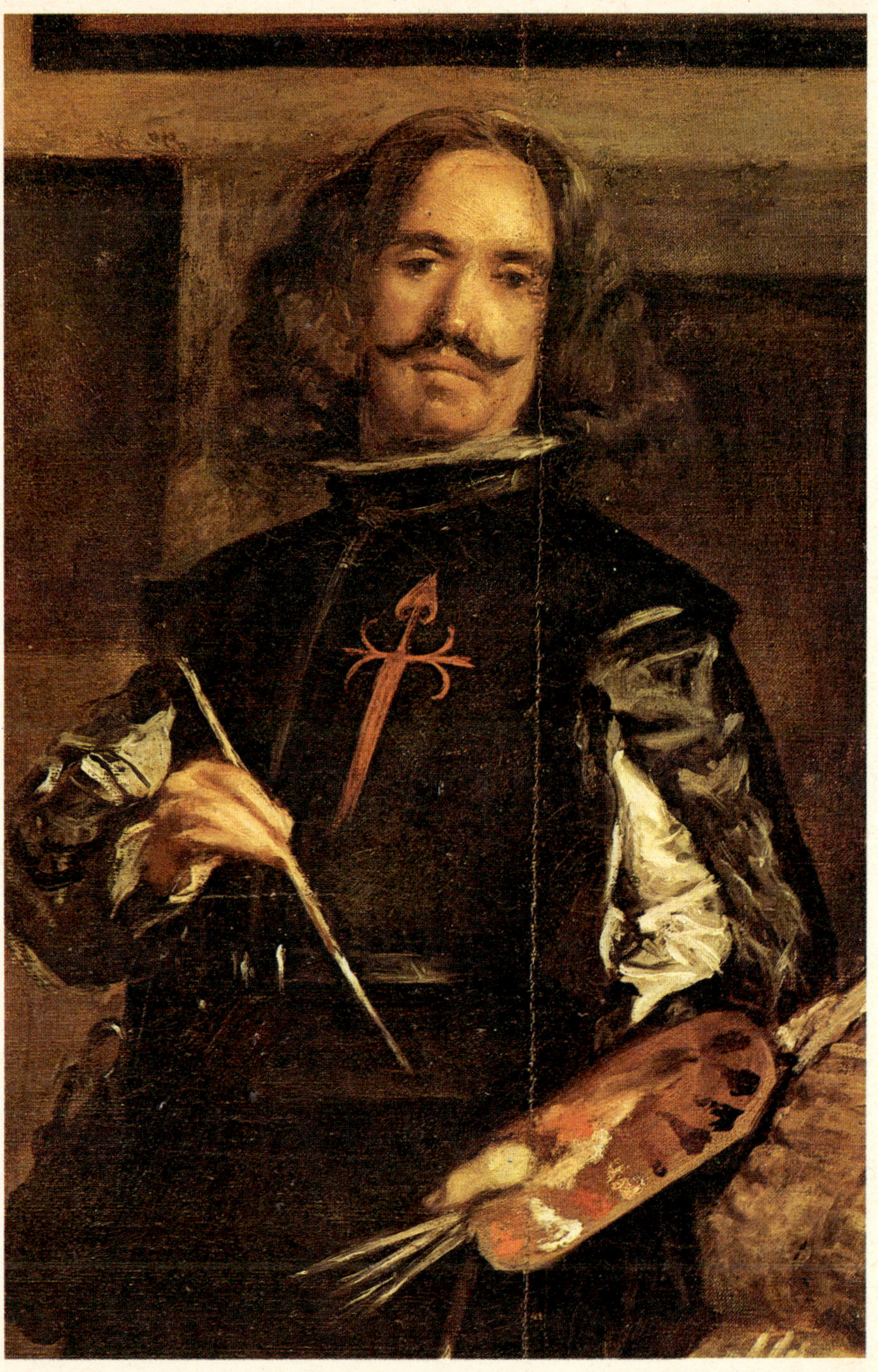

***The Maids of Honour** (**The Royal Family** or **Las Meninas**, **No. 123**).*
This is Velázquez' most famous painting and one of the finest examples of his personal approach to the artistic principles of the Baroque. He draws the spectator directly into the painting's space with no break in continuity between fiction and reality, his aim apparently being to capture a fleeting moment of the episode portrayed. All European art, from Goya to Manet, and to Picasso, owes something to this exceptional painting with its surprisingly modern sensibility.

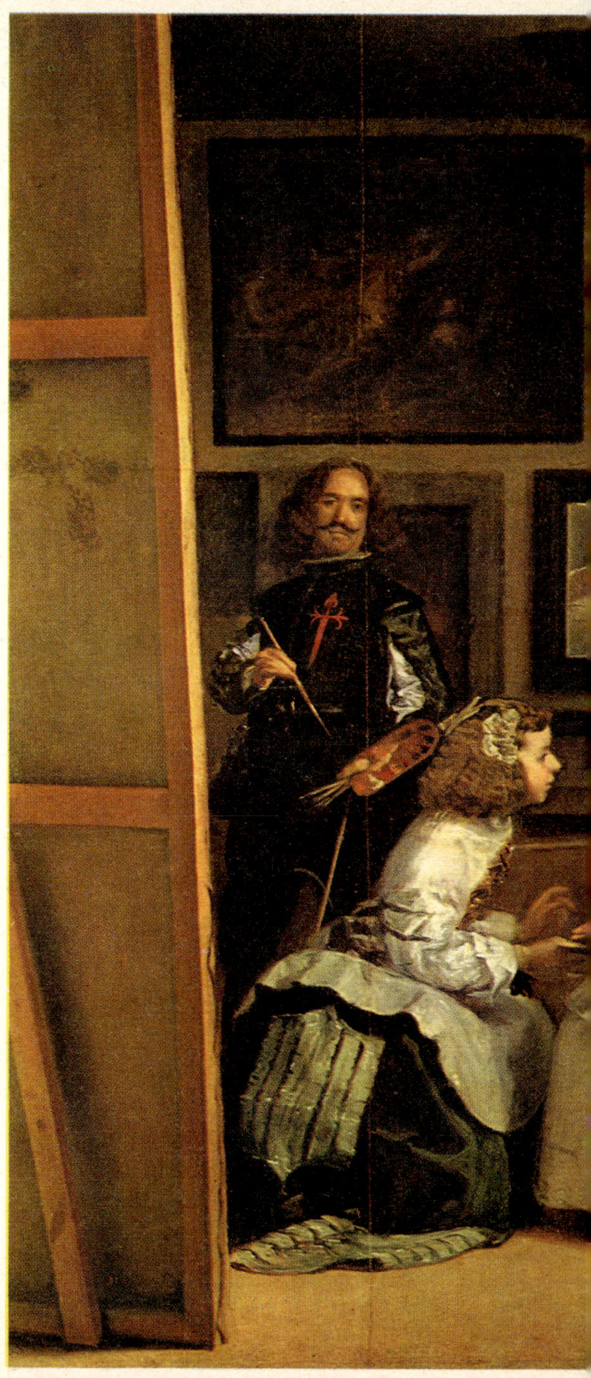

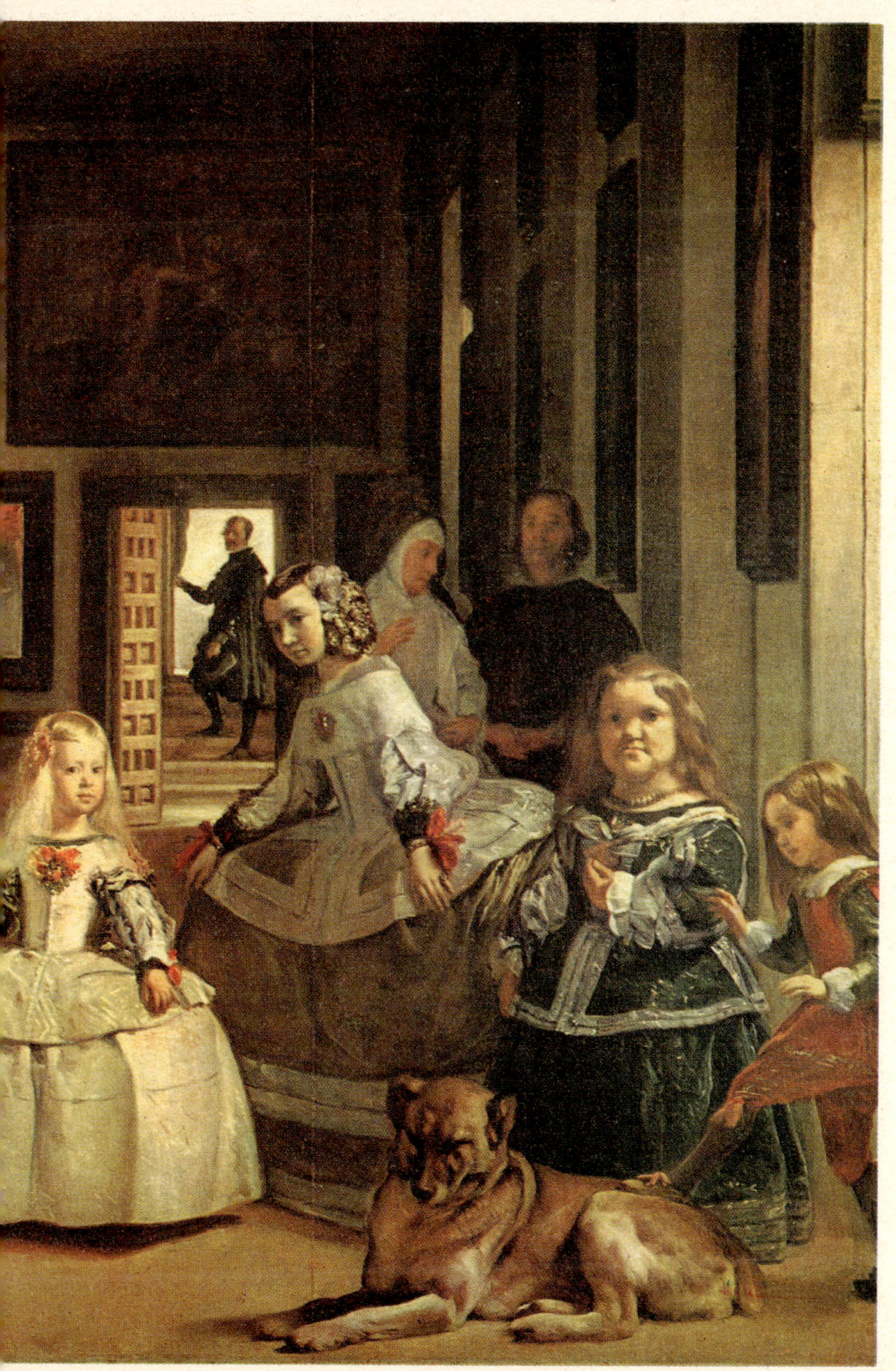

116 Queen Mariana
Oil on canvas/231 × 131/
1652 – 3
Madrid, Prado

117 The Infanta María Teresa
Oil on canvas/127 × 98.5/
1652–3
Vienna, Kunsthistorisches Museum

118 Philip IV *(bust)*
Oil on canvas/69 × 56/
1652–5
Madrid, Prado

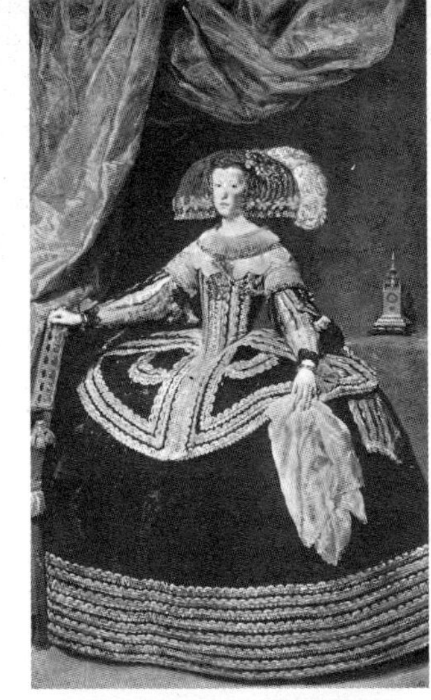

116

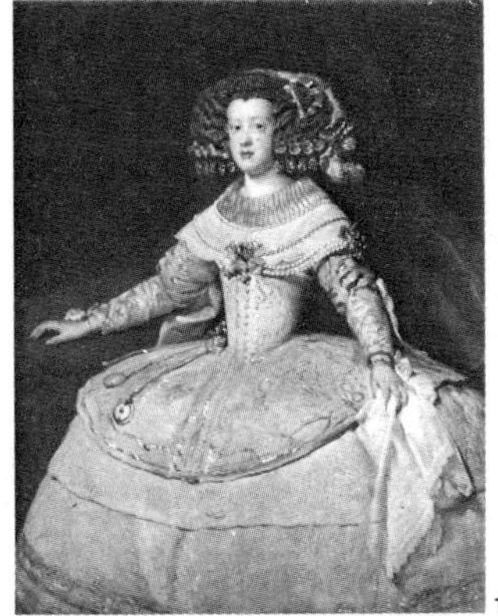

117

***The Fable of Arachne* (*No. 126, detail*).**

***The Fable of Arachne* (*Las Hilanderas, No. 126*)**
(pp. 86–7).
A delightful, vividly pictorial reinterpretation of the fable of Arachne from Ovid's Metamorphoses. *It is a good example of Velázquez' choice of chromatic solutions which clearly foreshadow the achievements of the French Impressionists and Pointillists during the latter half of the nineteenth century.*

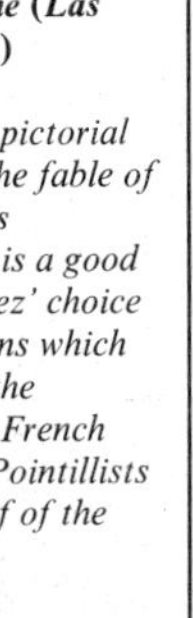

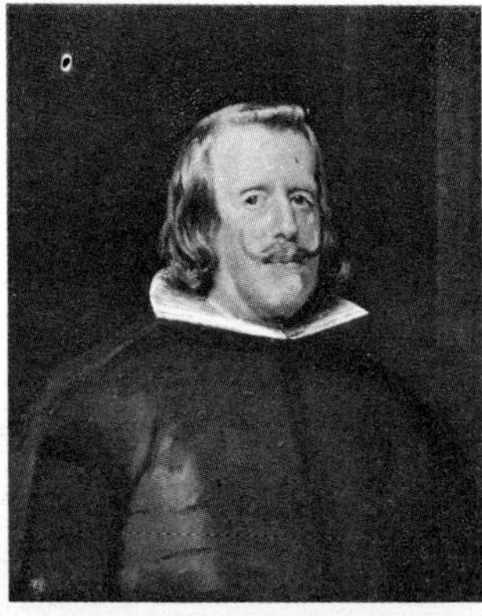

118

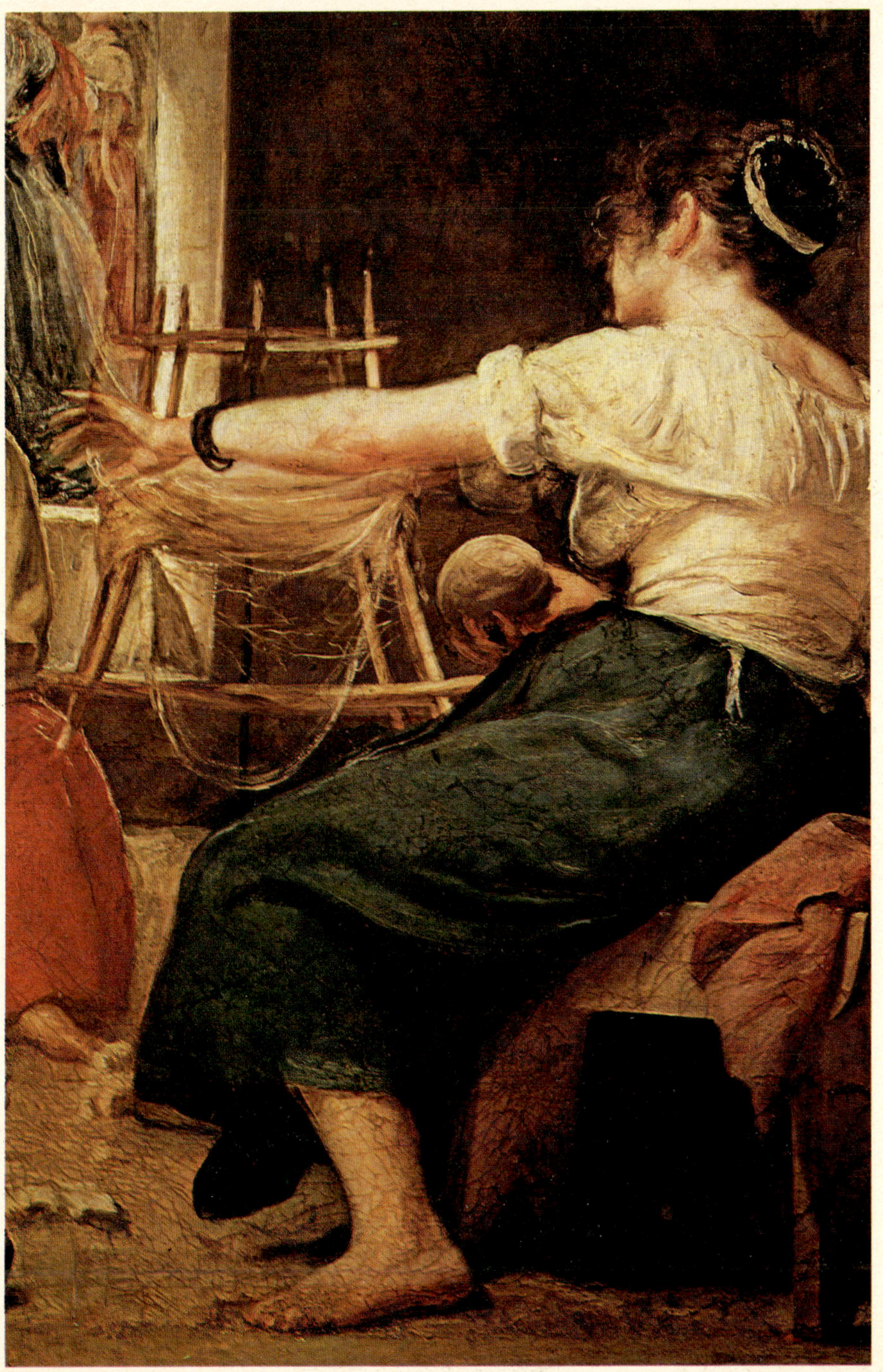

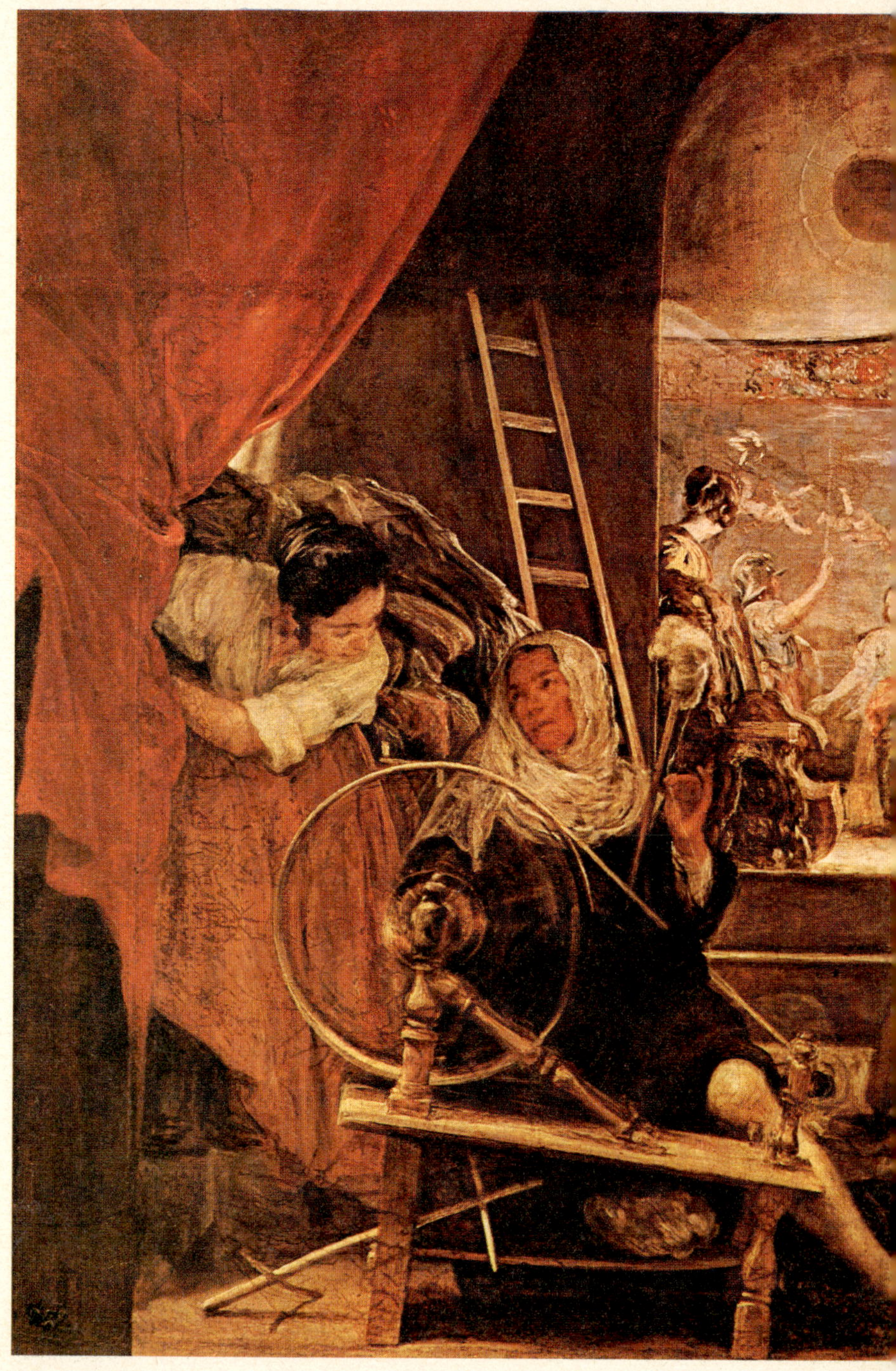

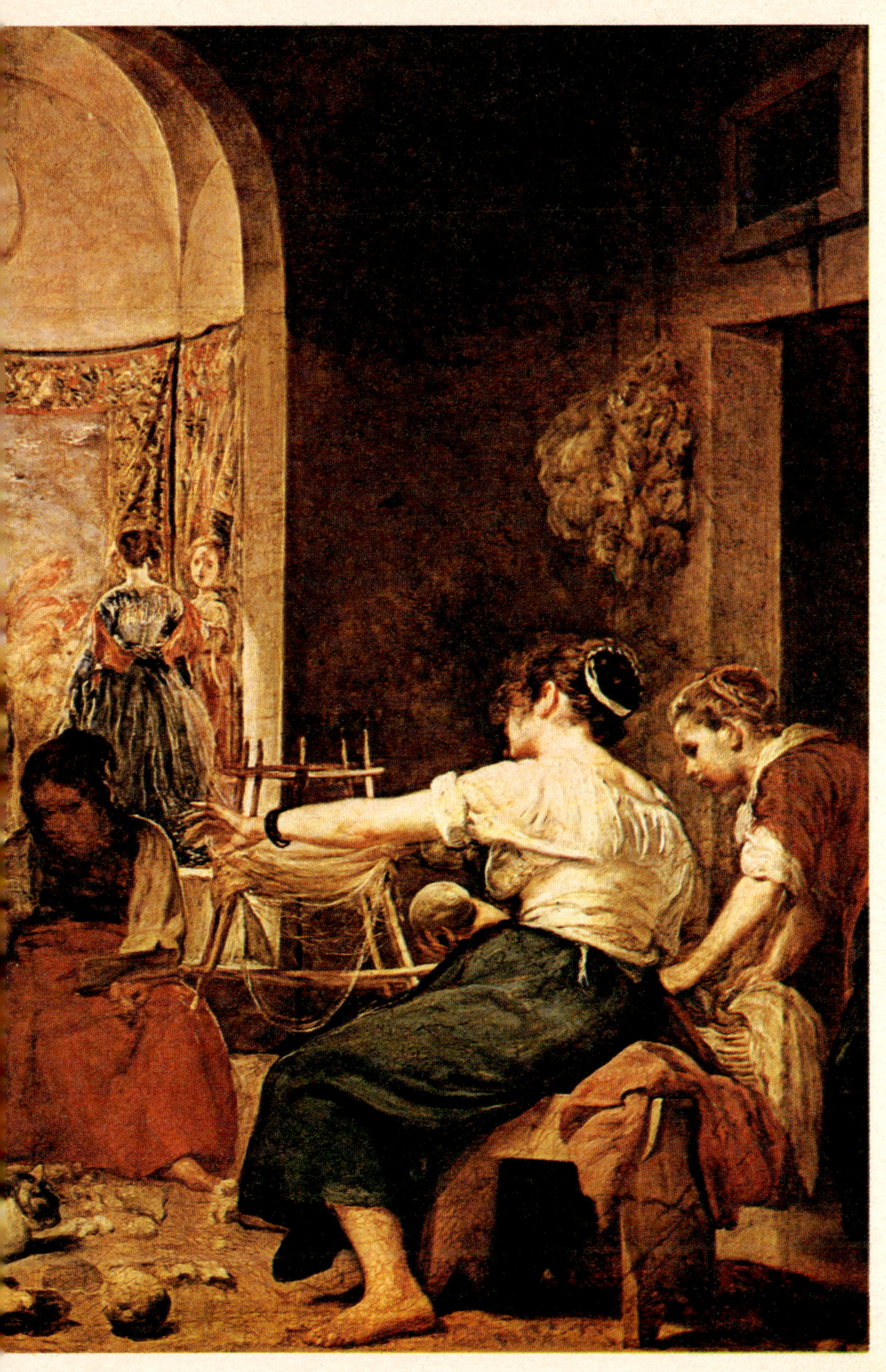

119 The Infanta Margarita
Oil on canvas/128.5 × 100/
1654 (?)
Vienna, Kunsthistorisches
Museum

120 The Infanta Margarita*
Oil on canvas/70 × 59/
1654 (?)
Paris, Louvre

121 The Infanta Margarita
Oil on canvas/47.5 × 39.4/
1654–5
New York, Art Market

122 The Infanta Margarita
Oil on canvas/105 × 88/1656
Vienna, Kunsthistorisches
Museum

***123 The Maids of Honour
('Las Meninas', 'The Royal
Family')***
Oil on canvas/318 × 276/1656
Madrid, Prado

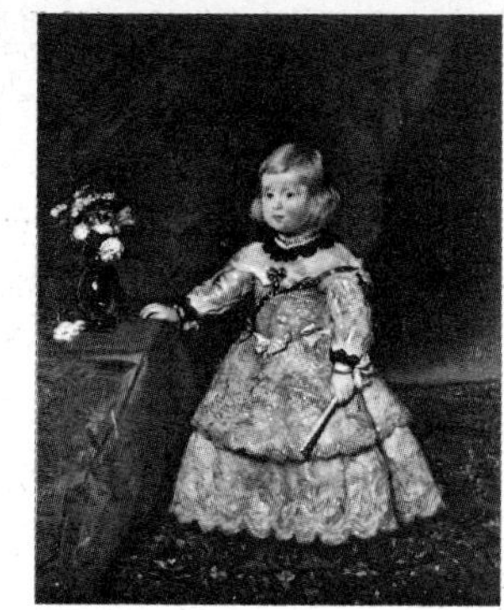
119

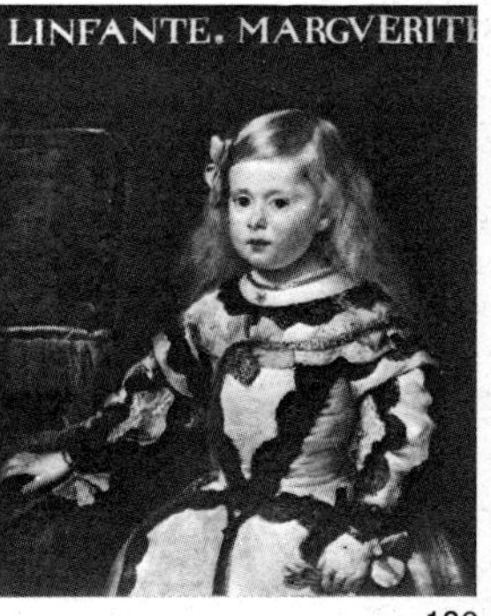

120

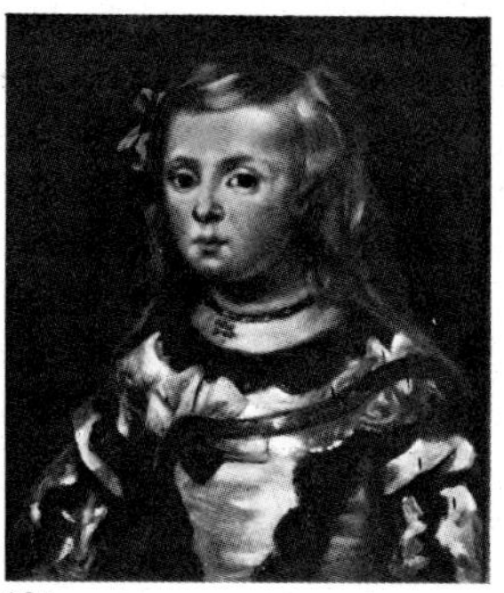
121

122
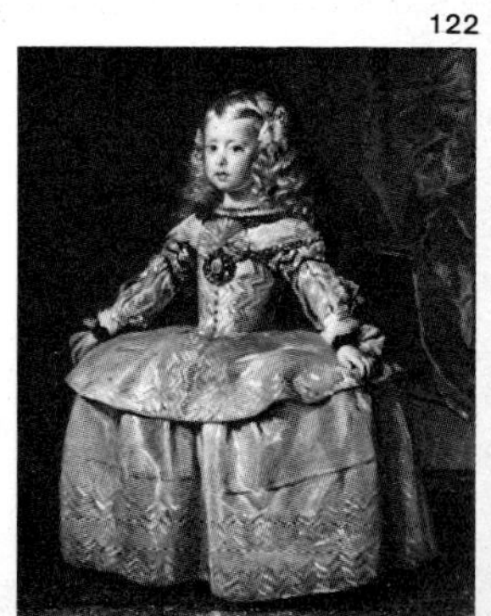

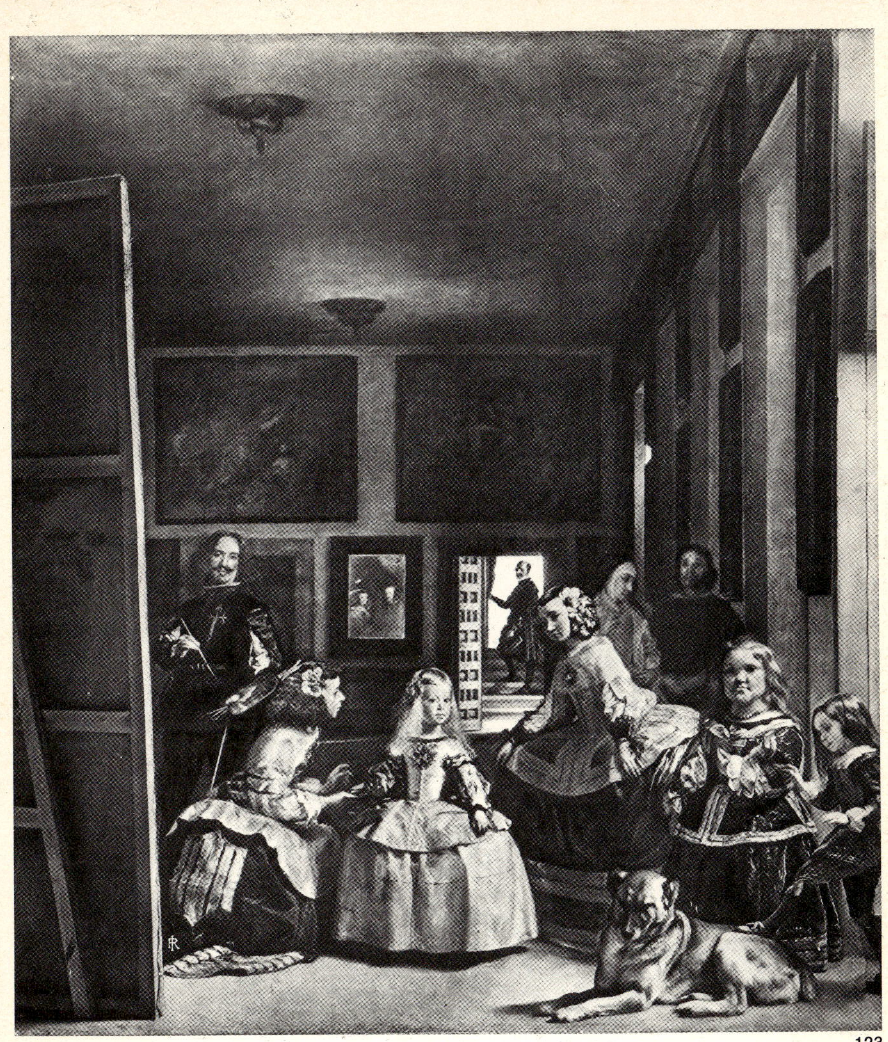

123

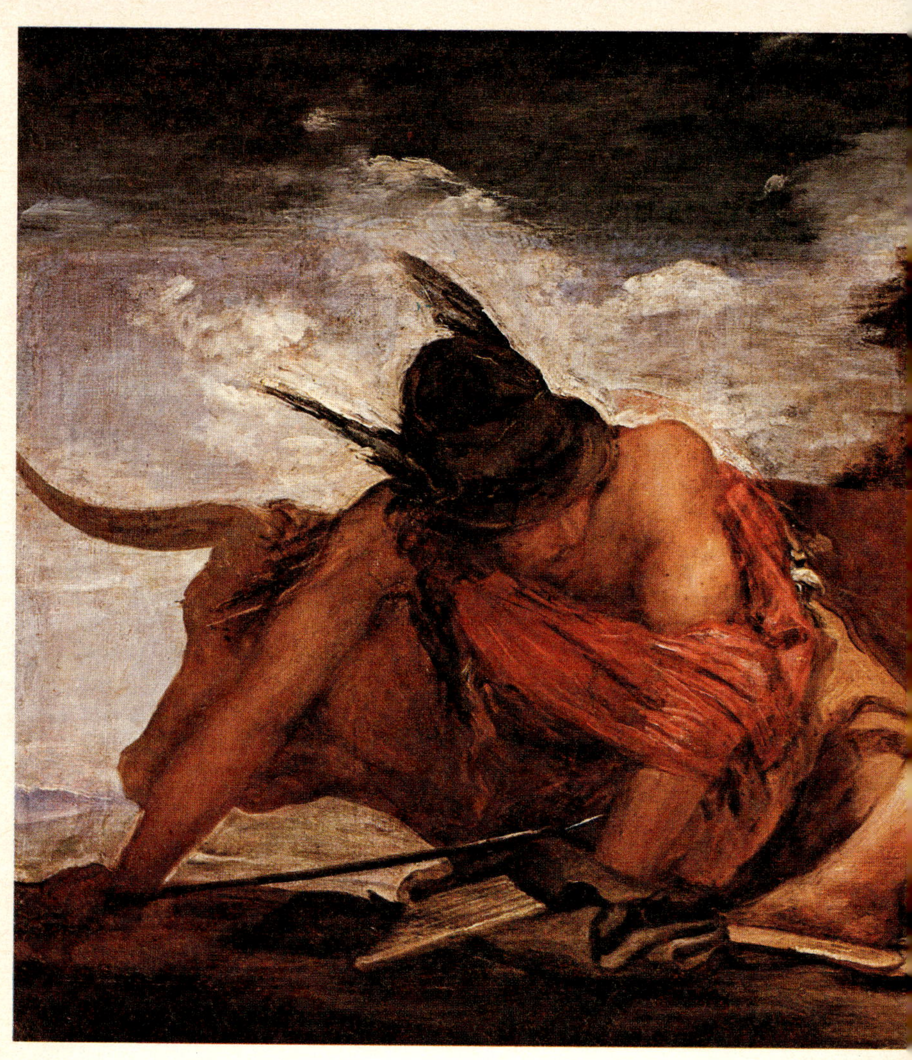

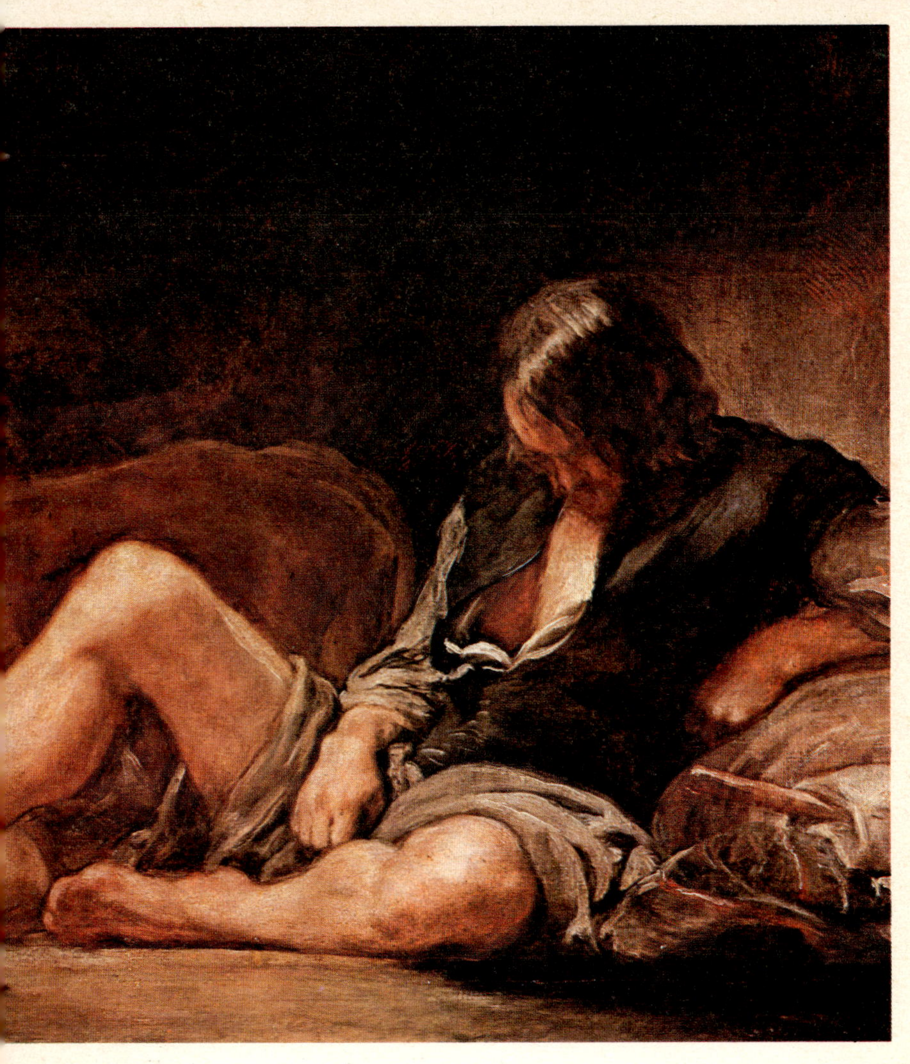

***Mercury and Argus* (No. 127).**
The figure of Argus, as scholars have pointed out, has precedents in Greek sculpture and Michelangelo's work. However, it is also true that when Velázquez chose subjects from antiquity he treated them simply as a scholarly pretext to be reinterpreted and subtly transformed into his own pictorial terms by his use of chromatic qualities. The earlier use of impasto has now given way to broad brush strokes of delicate colour.

124 Queen Mariana
Oil on canvas/46.5 × 43/1656
Paris, Rothschild Collection
Probably a study for No. 125

125 Queen Mariana
Oil on canvas/66 × 56/1656
Lugano, Thyssen-Bornemisza Collection

126 The Fable of Arachne ('Las Hilanderas')
Oil on canvas/220 × 289/1657 (?)
Madrid, Prado

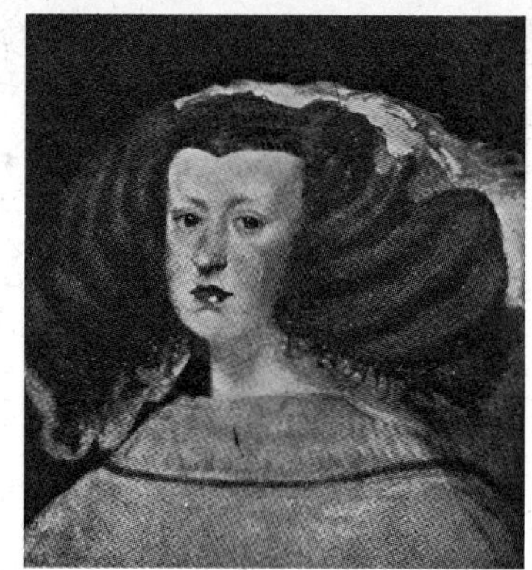
124

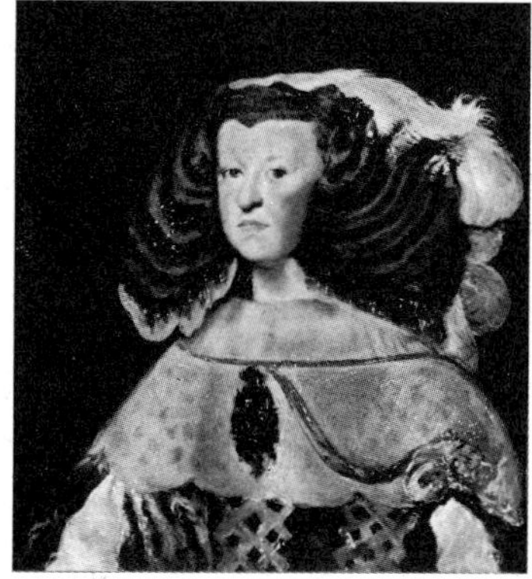
125

126
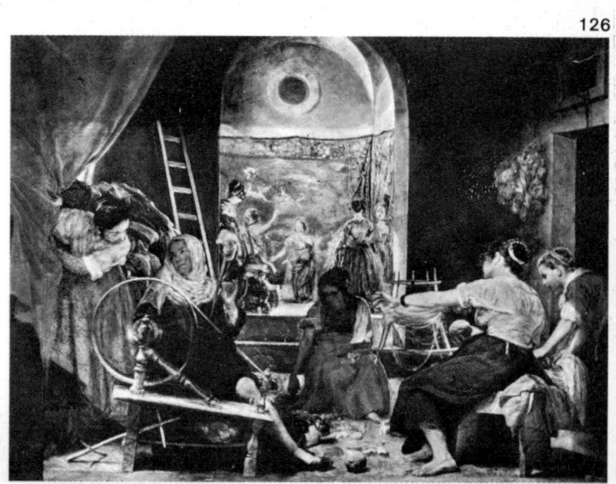

Prince Felipe Próspero (No. 128).
Although this painting has been damaged, especially at a level with the eyes, it is still one of Velázquez' finest last portraits both for its chromatic qualities (as in all his late works he makes extensive use of broad brush strokes of thin, almost transparent colour) and its evocation of shadowy space.

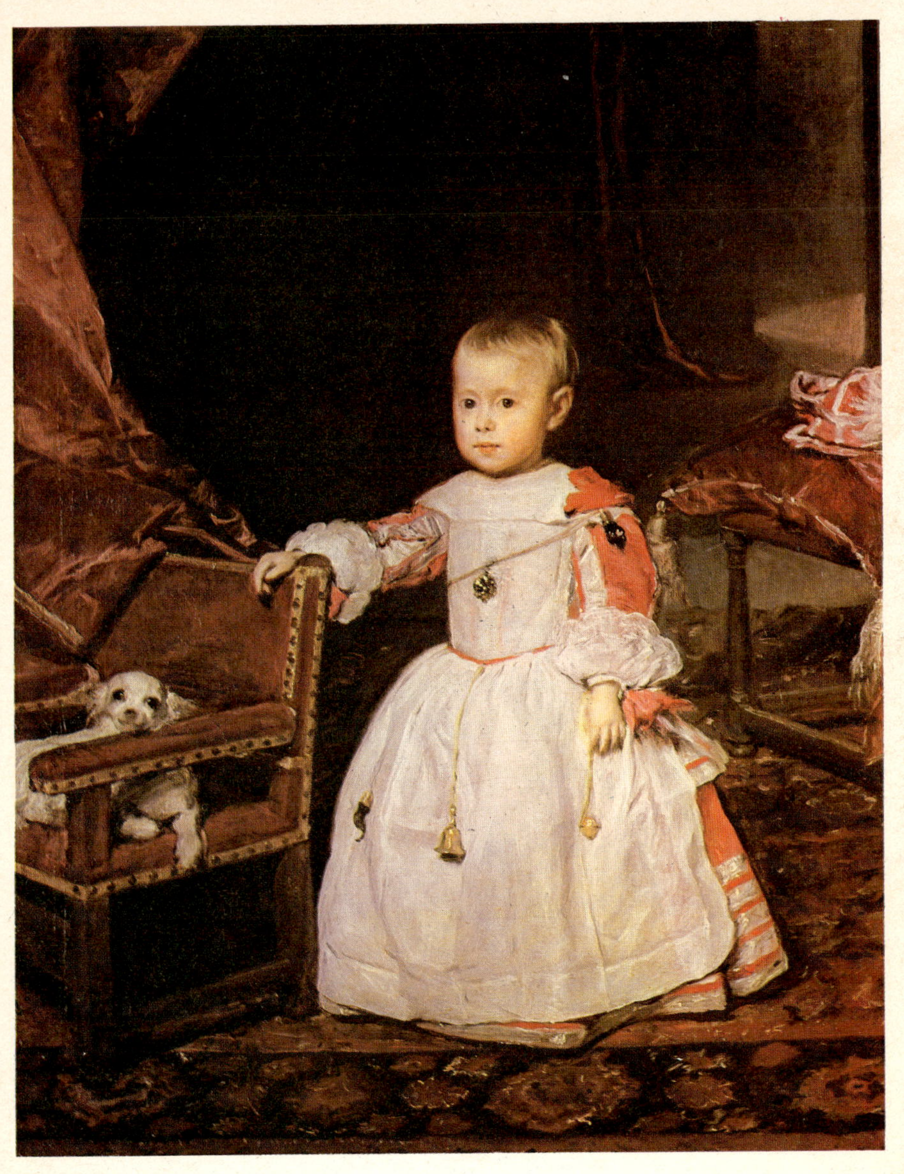

127 Mercury and Argus
Oil on canvas/127 × 248/1659
Madrid, Prado

128 Prince Felipe Próspero
Oil on board/128.5 × 99.5/
1659
Vienna, Kunsthistorisches
Museum

129 The Infanta Margarita
Oil on canvas/127 × 107/1659
Vienna, Kunsthistorisches
Museum

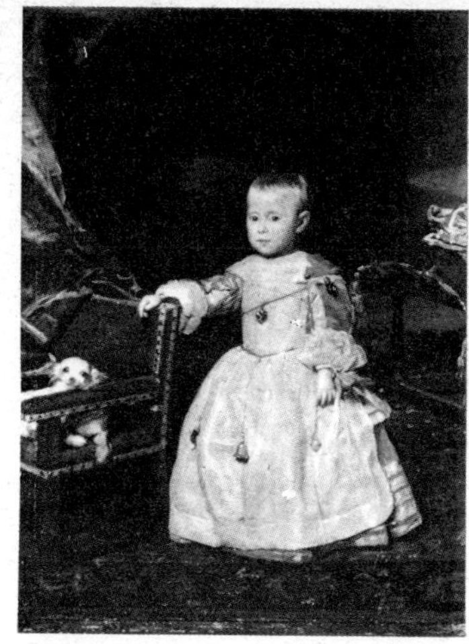
128

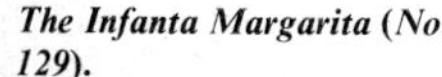

***The Infanta Margarita* (*No. 129*).**
The extraordinary range of transparent colour in this portrait (the exquisite rendering of the princess's rich dress, her white collar and sleeves impressionistically shot through with pale blue lights, her thick golden hair contrasting with the red wall hanging in the background) does not simply emphasize the work's explicit ceremonial purpose. It is the means by which the artist skilfully expresses in pictorial terms the air of regal solemnity which the little princess has already acquired.

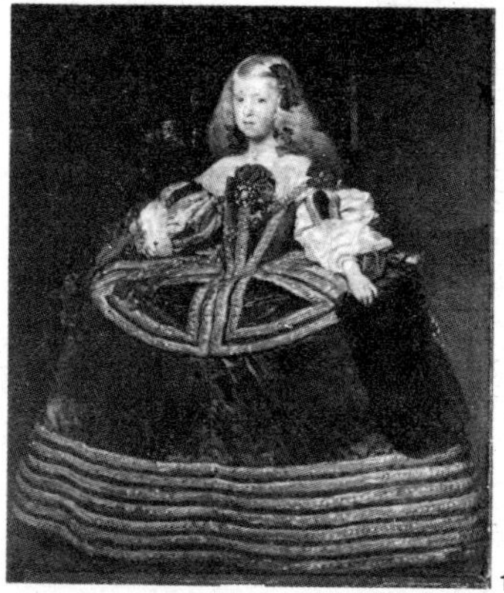
129

127
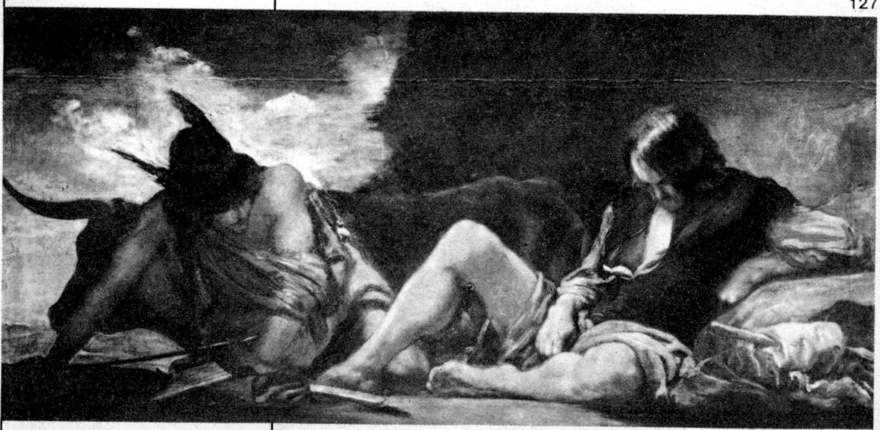